# The **Yo Momma** Vocabulary Builder

Classless Education Presents

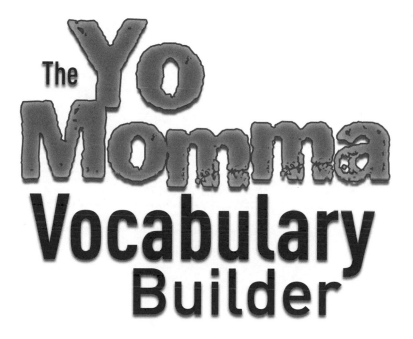

# The YO Momma Vocabulary Builder

**by Justin Heimberg,
Christopher Schultz,
and Steve Harwood**

**A Falls Media book**

Published by Falls Media
565 Park Ave, Suite 11E
New York, NY 10021

First Printing, April 2007

10 9 8 7 6 5 4 3 2

© Justin Heimberg, Christopher Schultz, and Steve Harwood, 2007

Printed in Canada

Design by Thomas Schirtz

ISBN-10: 0-9740439-8-2

ISBN-13: 978-0-9740439-8-2

**www.classlesseducation.com**

*To Our Mommus*

# Acknowledgements

The authors wish to thank David Miller, Chris Kyle, Jeff Sank, Keith Jones, Chris McAuliffe, Eric Immerman, Heidi Adams, and Allison Kor for their contributions. Thanks to Joe Mejia, who tackled the toughest copyediting questions with **alacrity** (see p. 116). Thanks to Terry Shelton for supplying many of the words in *Yo Momma*. Thanks to Aunt Sharon for being so **meticulous** (see p. 128). **Effusive** (see p. 39) thanks to Tom Schirtz, whose suffering provides us all with a healthy dose of **schadenfreude** (see p. 53). Tom, you truly maintain your **largesse** (see p. 6) and **equanimity** (see p. 118) amidst Fate's **mercurial** (see p. 123) hand. Thanks to the very **erudite** (see p. 29) Jon Stokes and his **masochistic** (see p. 41) **banter** (see p. 57) and for providing a cornucopia of humorous inspiration. Thanks to the **comely** (see p. 18) Lindsay Trout for her **esoteric** (see p. 142) knowledge of Warcraft. Steve would like to thank his darling **callipygian** (see p. 81) Amy, whose heart is as **Brobdingnagian** (see p. 8) as her **lexicon** (see p. 161). Justin would like to thank Marisa, for whom his **vehement** (see p. 106), **emphatic** (see p. 106) love and gratitude are **ineffable** (see p. 14).

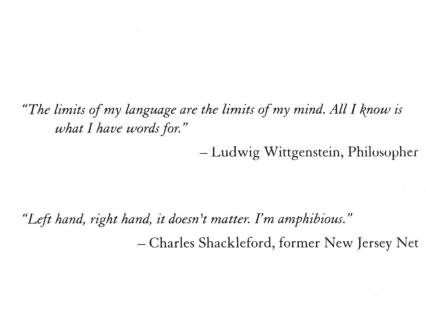

*"The limits of my language are the limits of my mind. All I know is what I have words for."*

— Ludwig Wittgenstein, Philosopher

*"Left hand, right hand, it doesn't matter. I'm amphibious."*

— Charles Shackleford, former New Jersey Net

# "Making Learning Bearable"

## A Message from The Board of Classless Education

Is there anything more gag-inducing than old people trying to act cool? I still remember a particularly painful high school assembly that featured failed musicians "rocking out" about the virtues of recycling: "One bucket for trash; one for paper, one for glass...." I was embarrassed for them, for me, for the audience, for the entire human race, and for any deity who had a part in our creation.

No one from the Board of Classless Education claims to be cool. We tuck our shirts in. We do, however, believe that learning should not be a torturous endeavor. Consequently, in this book there are no five-page rants about word origins that cite dead languages. Nor will you find examples of word usage from 19th century Victorian literature, or pronunciation symbols that look like something out of the Klingon alphabet.

We have three problems with the vocabulary-building texts out there:

1. They don't explain their words: That is, you'll get a definition, maybe a sample sentence, but nothing more. Nothing to explain how actually to use a word.

2. Their pronunciations are impossible to decipher, so even if you learn how to read a word, you still don't feel comfortable saying it.

3. They aren't funny.

So we decided to put the "fun" back in "underfunded educational system." *The Yo Momma Vocabulary Builder* is not just an educational book. It's also entertaining. It's *"edutainment."* And it's not just for students: It's generally informative, and anyone can benefit from reading it. It's *"Infoedutainment."* But let's be honest: We're also trying to make money off of it. So let's call it *"Adverinfoedutainment."* There. You just learned another word.

One serious point about increasing your vocabulary: Learning new words is about learning new ideas. And learning new ideas is inherently enriching: It allows you to express yourself more clearly and accurately. The primary reason to seek a larger vocabulary has nothing to do with impressing people, cultivating professional gain, or building scholarly achievement. Rather, increasing the words and ideas at your disposal deepens and broadens your understanding of the world, of others, and of yourself. It makes life more interesting. Sorry to be so **didactic** (see p. 139).

Now, let's get bizzay with some off-the-chain word power! Internet!

*Justin Heimberg*
*President, Board of Classless Education*

## The Real Origin of **Yo Momma**

A common misconception is that the game known as "Snaps," aka "The Dozens," aka "Yo Momma," originated on the streets of America's inner cities. The truth is that Yo Momma battles existed long before street culture brought the phenomenon into the mainstream.

As early as the turn of the 19th century, an underground society of intellectuals battled in library basements, university quads and faculty conference rooms, belittling each other's mothers with **grandiloquent** (see p. 75) verbal jabs. Luckily, these tree-lined street poets were scholars, and for scholars, it's **obligatory** (see p. 95) to write down their every thought. Consequently, there were many yo momma snaps to choose from. Scores of researchers pored over countless volumes of scholarly tomes, culling from them a compendium of **erudite** (see p. 29) **pejoratives** (see p. 140). Thus was *The Yo Momma Vocabulary Builder* born. And now, without **superfluous** (see p. 86) ado, it's time to turn the page and learn from **Yo Momma**. . . .

# Yo momma's so **ubiquitous**, when she sits around the house, she sits AROUND the house!

**u·biq·ui·tous** (yoo BIK wi tuhs)
adj. Being or seeming to be everywhere at the same time

**Ubiquitous** does not mean fat or huge, but rather "seemingly everywhere." Paris Hilton is ubiquitous. Jerry Bruckheimer is ubiquitous: It seems like his name is attached to every movie or TV show that comes out. Ubiquitous advertising helped turn the iPod into a phenomenon. Nothing is more ubiquitous than Starbucks: You can't walk ten feet without hitting one. Starbucks is so ubiquitous that one day, you might see a Starbucks in the Lincoln Memorial, or in your home, or even in another Starbucks. **Ubiquity** or **ubiquitousness** is the noun, though both are anything but ubiquitous: You rarely see the noun form.


# Yo momma's so **emaciated**, she can hula hoop in a fruit loop.

**e·ma·ci·a·ted** (i MAY shee ay tid)
adj. Very thin, especially from disease, hunger, or cold

**Emaciated** isn't just skinny. It's too skinny, unhealthy-looking, skeletal. Think Olsen twins, supermodels, Gollum from *Lord of the Rings*, and Ally McBeal. Gandhi's hunger strike left him emaciated. In Hollywood, there are a lot of "hunger strikes without the causes," so to speak, spurring some social critics to declare that we live in an "Emaciation Nation." The dying, withering-away look has become in vogue, a trend that could make you conclude that America's soul is currently emaciated.

# **Your momma's** skin is so **pallid**, snowflakes leave stain marks.

**pal·lid** (PAL id)
  adj.  Pale, usually as a result of poor health; lacking vitality

The good thing about the word "**pallid**" is that it resembles the word "pale," and it actually means "pale."  Normally, a question like that on the SAT tries to trick you by offering a multiple choice answer that sounds like the word, but actually isn't the right definition.  They'll give you "**noisome**" and you'll think it means "loud," but it actually means "foul-smelling, **fetid** (see p. 15)." You get so fed up, you start filling in the answer sheet "DC CAB, DC CAB" and so on.  But pallid is pale and, as such, can mean "lacking in radiance or vitality; dull" (pallid prose, for example).

# **Yo momma's** so **hirsute**, she bathes with a Rug Doctor!

**hir·sute** (hur SUIT or HUR suit)
  adj.  Hairy; covered with hairs

The easiest way to remember what **hirsute** means is to think of "hair suit."  It means hairy.  Very hairy.  King Kong is hirsute. Austin Powers got a lot of comic mileage with an overly hirsute chest.  Since he was a character unfrozen from the 1960's, he was convinced that women loved his **hirsuteness**, but alas, it's a new millennium, and being **depilated** (see p. 88) is what's attractive now.  The character Borat has hirsute thighs, two words you seldom want to see together.

### Sampling:

*The hair-caked drains in college dorm showers sickened the cleaning staff, though the drains were nothing compared to the communal bars of soap, so **hirsute** they resembled SOS pads.*

# Yo momma's so **voracious**,
## her blood type's Ragu.

**vo·ra·cious** (vuh RAY shus)
adj. Wanting vast quantities of food; having a huge appetite for anything

If your momma has a **voracious** appetite, she is always hungry. She looks at the menu and says "yes." She eats Wheat Thicks. In a more general sense, voracious can mean having a rampant appetite for any pursuit or activity. Yo momma could devour crossword puzzles **voraciously**. Cereal mascots have insanely voracious appetites for their product, almost to the point of addiction.[1] You often hear the term "voracious reader" to describe someone who devours books—figuratively speaking, of course. You seldom hear the term "voracious television watcher," though, in truth, there are far more of those.

If yo momma is so voracious, yo momma is likely to become so **corpulent** that she has to put her belt on with a boomerang (see next page). And if yo momma is voracious, she is also synonymously **rapacious**, **ravenous**, and **gluttonous**. Note: If yo momma is so **veracious** (with an "e"), she is truthful, and the only thing she has a voracious appetite for is truth-telling.

---

1 *Note: Recent studies suggest that the Cocoa Puffs bird's addiction to Cocoa Puffs is largely* **psychosomatic** *(affected by the mind), as he was found to go cuckoo for a placebo in laboratory tests.*

**Yo momma's** so **corpulent**, when her beeper goes off, people think she's backing up.

**cor·pu·lent** (CORE pyoo luhnt)
adj. Excessively fat, portly, stout

**Corpulence** is a growing problem with today's youth, according to many recent studies. Here's a quick test: If the sports you play involve hand controls and looking at a TV screen, you might be at risk of becoming **corpulent**. Many sitcoms feature corpulent men orbited by beautiful **emaciated** (see p. 1) women. Just like in real life. Despite its meaning, there is something polite-sounding about the word corpulent, making this insult sound almost dignified. It just goes to show you that the sound of a word, as well as its meaning, can create effect.

**See how the overall effects of the phrases below change when you substitute "corpulent" for "fat."**

- Corpulent Albert
- *Rush Limbaugh is a Big Corpulent Idiot*
- George Forman's Lean Mean Corpulence Reducing Grilling Machine
- Corpulent Burger
- *Jake and the Corpulent Man*
- Shut up, or I'll give you a corpulent lip!
- *My Big Corpulent Greek Wedding*
- 80's rap trio "The Corpulent Boys"
- Chinese action star "Chow Yun-Corpulent"

# **Yo-Yo Ma** is so **fat**, he has to hold his breath to play his cello.

Wait a second. That's not right. These are "yo momma" jokes, not "Yo-Yo Ma" jokes. Shoot, we always get those confused! For those of you who are **philistines** (see p. 57), Yo-Yo Ma is a renowned classical cellist. We just made a particular kind of mistake. We've committed what's called a **malapropism**.

> **mal·a·prop·ism** (MAL uh prop iz uhm)
> n. Ridiculous misuse of a word, especially by confusing it with one that sounds similar

A **malapropism** is so called after Mrs. Malaprop, a character noted for her amusing misuse of words in a play you'll never see by a person you don't need to know about. Examples of malapropism can be found in the character Ali G's request "Let's talk about a very *tattoo* subject" (i.e. "taboo") or, proving fact is funnier than fiction, in Mike Tyson's genius idiocy: "I might just fade into *Bolivian*, you know what I mean?" (i.e. "**oblivion**," see p. 24).

### Other **Yo-Yo Ma** snaps:

**Yo-Yo Ma** is so stupid, he took in his cello to be repaired because they told him his music was Baroque!

**Yo-Yo Ma** is so short, he needs a crossbow to reach his strings!

**Yo-Yo Ma** is so ugly, he should live under his bridge!

**Yo-Yo Ma** is so old, he played live accompaniment for Schubert!

**Yo-Yo Ma** is so fat, he sat down, and the orchestra skipped!

**Yo momma** possesses such **largesse**,
she'd give me the hair off her back.

**lar·gesse** (lar JESS)
   n. Generosity in gift-giving

No, this word is not related to **hirsute** (see p. 2). Someone who
displays **largesse** is always giving stuff to people or to causes. (It
can also be spelled without the last "e," good news if your hand gets
tired toward the end.) Although it doesn't have to be used this way,
there's often an implied degree of showiness handcuffed to largesse,
something Trumpian and flamboyant about the generosity. As in,
nobody disputes the value of your gift, buddy, but somehow this
gift seems to be more about you than the recipient. Consider the
largesse of political lobbyists, who give billions of dollars to political
honchos in hopes of cultivating favorable legislation for their many
causes. Or take Sean Penn giving his time to help Hurricane
Katrina victims, while his publicist just happened to be around to
record his noble largesse. Below is a **mnemonic** (ni MAHN ik) to
help you remember what largesse means. A mnemonic is any
device or trick to help you remember something.

**Yo Mnomma's Mnemonics:**

*The "large 'S'" stands for:*

# S
   ometimes
   hady
   elflessness

**Yo momma** is so **egregiously** stupid,
   she told me to meet her on the corner of Walk and
   Don't Walk.

**e·gre·gious** (i GREE juhs)
   adj. Horrifically terrible, shockingly bad

**Egregious** means the worst of the worst. If you're an egregious
liar, you are the worst kind of liar. New Coke was an egregious
marketing mistake. Janet Jackson had an egregious wardrobe
malfunction at the 2004 Super Bowl. Michael Jackson showed an
egregious lapse of judgment when he dangled his baby over a
hotel balcony in Paris. (We could go through the whole Jackson
family and effectively demonstrate uses of the word egregious,
but let's move on.) Author James Frey tangled himself in a web
of egregious deceit by claiming his work of fiction, *A Million
Little Pieces*, was a memoir. Mel Gibson's drunken comments
about Judaism were **egregiously** offensive. And speaking of…

## Five egregious misspellings of Hanukkah:

- Chanukaha
- Ghananka
- Chunkyka
- Honkeykah
- Donkeykong

**Sampling:**

*Thomas looked in the mirror at his tattoo of a life-size Fats
Domino head and realized he had made an* **egregious** *mistake.*

# Yo momma's so ugly, her psychiatrist makes her lie **prostrate**!

**pros·trate** (PRAHS trayt)
adj.  Lying face-down and flat; helpless; exhausted
v.  To fling oneself down as if in submission; to make helpless; to exhaust physically

Picture *COPS* on TV.  Sometimes when they catch shirtless bad guys, they force them face-down on the ground before handcuffing them.  That position, pre-cuffing, is a **prostrate** one, or one of **prostration**.  Sometimes, the criminal will prostrate himself since he knows the cops have guns and pepper spray.  There can also be a more figurative meaning to signify that a certain person, group, or situation has been crippled or exhausted: "Legend has it that Led Zeppelin prostrated the staff of pretty much every hotel they stayed in."

# Yo momma's so **Brobdingnagian**, when she tripped over 4th Ave., she landed on 12th!

**Brob·ding·nag·i·an** (brahb ding NAG ee uhn)
adj.  Immense, gigantic

We just went Swiftian on you, yo!  In Jonathan Swift's book *Gulliver's Travels*, Gulliver visits an island called Brobdingnag, where everything is so big, he's in constant danger.  So relatively **diminutive** (see p. 40) is Gulliver,  he gets attacked by rats that are as big as dogs, and the cries of babies are deafening to him.  He also, predictably, has zero luck with the ladies, though a nine-year-old girl keeps him out of danger.  The word easily slipped from Swift's book into common usage by adding "-ian" to make it an **eponymous** (see p. 62) adjective.

# Yo momma's such a **Luddite**, you told her you wanted a Playstation, and she got you a tree house!

**Lud·dite** (LUDD ite)
n. Someone who is against technological innovation and progress

Examples of **Luddites** abound: a friend who refuses to get a cell phone, for instance, or a person who hand-writes essays rather than using a computer. Remember the Unabomber, the Harvard-educated American terrorist? He sent bombs through the mail to people he thought were hurting the world because of the technological advancements they'd helped make happen. He finally was arrested in a cabin in the middle of nowhere, making him the Luddite of our times. The term "Luddite" is capitalized because it comes from the surname of Ned Ludd, the Unabomber of his day. Ludd, an English laborer, fearing rampant unemployment for his blue-collar kinsmen, sabotaged then cutting-edge weaving machinery around 1779.

### L.I.T. (Luddite Institute of Technology) Sample Course Curriculum

**21.340 Introduction to String Theory** - This course explores the differences between string, twine and rope.

**24.410 Computer Aerodynamics** - This course explores the many ways to throw a computer: across-the-room tosses, computer **defenestrations** (see p. 91), even computer-at-computer hurls.

**21.770 Dancing to Acapella** - This course explores the foundations of hip-hop dancing without resorting to using a "boom box," "turntable," or other modern audio devices. Note: This course does NOT teach "The Robot."

**22.920 Hands-On Net Work Optimization** - This hands-on course is meant to maximize the efficiency of your net making. Students will make fishing nets, butterfly nets, and larger fishing nets. Prerequisite Course: Introduction to String Theory.

# Yo momma's so **granacious**, she married young just to get the rice!

**gra·na·cious** (gruh NAY shuhs)

adj. "Looking for grains"; uninterested in solutions and whole truths; curious, but only to a degree

Someone who is **granacious** craves grains of things. He is interested only in kernels of ideas. We all know the granacious type, the person who is always looking to understand just a little bit of a subject, but not too much (a **dilettante**, a dabbler). Actually, this is a completely made-up word. There is no such thing as "granacious." We are being **duplicitous**, or deceitful, and if you believed us, you were **credulous**, or believing, gullible, overly-trusting, naïve. If you doubted this word from the get-go, congratulations: You were *incredulous*.

If you are incredulous, you are skeptical; you are unwilling or unable to believe something, even if it's true. Perhaps it is because you find what you are hearing to be too in*cred*ible to be true. Or perhaps the person telling you doesn't have enough street *cred* to be believable. He doesn't have the *cred*entials. You question their *cred*ibility while you use your *cred*it card…. You get the point: It all comes from the Latin root *credere*, "to believe." Here are some facts that might make you incredulous:

- There are more plastic flamingos in the U.S. than real ones

- In one year, more Monopoly money is printed than real money

- The reason quarters have grooves on their edges is because they were once used as gears in times of war

OK, so that last one was fake. It is a **specious** explanation. For more specious facts, turn to page 35.

# Yo momma is da bomma!

And consequently, she is a **portmanteau**.

**port·man·teau** (port man TOE)
n. A word made from blending two or more words

"Bomma" is an example of merging two words—da "bomb" and "momma"—into one, and a word made from two words fused together is a **portmanteau**. Smoke + fog = smog. Breakfast + lunch = brunch. If you know any rich kids living off trust funds who nonetheless don't wash their hair and wear torn jeans and tie-dyes, you might label them the portmanteau "trustafarian." Modern day usage of portmanteau can be found in descriptions of Hollywood supercouples Bennifer, Brangelina, and TomKat. But Lewis Carroll of *Alice In Wonderland* fame beat the gossip writers to the idea with words like "chortle" (chuckle + snort).

**Unlikely Hollywood portmanteau super couples:**

- Dobberts (Lou Dobbs and Julia Roberts)
- BobCat (Bob Saget and Catherine Zeta Jones)
- LoHanSolo (Lindsey Lohan and Harrison Ford)
- AguiLarry (Christina Aguilera and Larry Holmes)
- Phillary (Dr. Phil and Hillary Duff)
- BoutrosBoutrosHalle (Boutros Boutros-Ghali and Halle Berry)
- Portmanto (Natalie Portman and Tony Danza)

**Some portmanteaux[1] you'll never see anywhere other than this book:**

- Blappy – When you feel bloated and also happy
- Bumbrella – Any hobo that prevents you from getting wet
- Bananadana – A banana peel tied around the forehead or neck
- Pimplode – To date excessively, to the point no one wants to go out with you anymore

1. *As if the French "portmanteau" weren't pretentious enough, although a simple "s" is fine, you can pluralize it with an "x."*

# Yo momma's so **sesquipedalian**, by the time she finishes telling a bedtime story, it's time to wake up.  Look it up, fool!!!

**ses·qui·pe·da·li·an** (ses kwi puh DAYl yn)
adj. Having many syllables; characterized by long words
(as in a piece of writing or speech)

**Sesquipedalian** means using long words.  Or it can be used to describe a word of many syllables.  And sesquipedalian, of course, is a sesquipedalian word itself.  It's an example of what it means.  And that's just cool.  Obviously you would never use this word in everyday conversation.  If you did, you would be whimpering sesquipedalian last words as people pummeled you to death.  But like an expensive wine, it's a word you can uncork every once in a while and savor with a group of your most pretentious friends.

## Quizzle

Match the **sesquipedalian** word with its meaning:

**(word)**

- Pneumonoultramicroscopicsilicovolcanoconiosis
- Honorificabilitudinitatibus
- Supercalifragilisticexpialidocious
- Floccinaucinihilipilification

**(meaning)**

- Honorableness
- A lung disease caused by breathing in particles of siliceous volcanic dust
- An estimation of something as worthless
- A word nannies use to enchant children's impressionable minds

*Answer: Does it really matter? (Pardon our floccinaucinihilipilification.)*

# Yo momma's so **unctuous**, her freckles slipped off.

**unc·tu·ous** (UNGK choo us)
adj. Having an oily or soapy feel; excessively smooth, suave, or smug; insincerely earnest

**Unctuous** can mean slippery or oily (if you're an oyster lover, it's the perfect word to describe them), but it is generally used to describe a person who is excessively smooth, someone who radiates insincere earnestness. Con artists are unctuous, used car salesmen are as unctuous as the cars they wax, and politicians are too often the **apotheosis** (see p. 85) of **unctuousness**. People's love-hate opinion of President Bill Clinton speaks to the fine subjective line between sincerity and unctuousness. (Did he really feel our pain?) Unctuous people are just too polished and ingratiating to trust. Think of Ryan Seacrest asking "you're-my-pal" questions to *American Idol* contestants, or, perhaps more accurately, the wannabe managers fawning over the finalists of the show, hoping to represent them as they sign big label deals.

**Unctuous or not? You decide.**

- John Edwards
- Carson Daly
- Arsenio Hall interviews
- 1980's game show hosts
- The laughter of *Entertainment Tonight* hosts
- James Lipton, host of *Inside the Actors Studio*
- Johnnie Cochran
- Gap employee greetings

**Yo momma** is so **ineffably** fat, she jumped up in the air and got stuck!

**in·ef·fa·ble** (in EFF uh buhl)
adj.  Unable to be expressed or described

Things that are **ineffable** cannot be expressed or described. The staggering idiocy of many modern Hollywood films is ineffable.  It is ineffably frustrating when your computer breaks and tech support puts you on hold.  Also, ineffable can mean "unable to be spoken," like the word "God" in some orthodox faiths.  In Harry Potter's universe, Lord Voldemort's name is ineffable to many superstitious wizards.  And to use a segue you don't hear much, "And speaking of wizards…"

**Yo momma's** neck is so **wizened**, she can grate cheese on it.

**wiz·ened** (WIZ und)
adj. Withered, shriveled, or wrinkled, usually by age

An easy way to remember this word is by thinking of an old wizard with wrinkled features: "wizened wizards." Wizened means withered and shriveled.  In order to have the **gravitas** (see p. 17) wizards need, they must cultivate their wizened looks, spending long days in the sun, avoiding moisturizer and squinting a lot.  Great wizened figures (which would make a good stamp line, incidentally) include Yoda, Gandalf, and the California Raisins.  Many of Hollywood's aging starlets have their faces surgically unwizened (to coin a word), but they can do nothing about their wizened necks, thus accounting for the booming ascot industry.  Have you ever seen an old man so wrinkled, he looked like he had corduroy skin?  That's wizened.

**Yo momma's** pits are so **fetid**, she slowed down Speed Stick!

**fet·id** (FET id)
adj. Having an offensive odor

Let's see, she also made Right Guard turn left and made Secret go public. What else? She made Old Spice die. And, uh, she made Sure reconsider. Those are all the deodorant jokes we've got. **Fetid** means foul-smelling, malodorous. New York City dumpsters are fetid. In New Orleans, the air around Bourbon Street the morning after a Mardi Gras parade is fetid. You know the guy who never took his gym shirt home until it crusted with sweat and grime, eventually adopting the consistency of aluminum foil? That shirt and that guy's locker are fetid. If yo momma is fetid, she is synonymously **putrid**, **noisome**, and, to invoke slang, **funky**. **Pungent** means strong-smelling (good or bad), and **redolent** generally suggests a pleasant or at least tolerable smell.

**Yo momma's** so **redundant**, it took her 2 hours to watch *60 Minutes*.

**re·dun·dant** (ri DUHN dunt)
adj. Characterized by unnecessary repetition; no longer useful, unnecessary

When you combine two phrases or words together when one will do, that's **redundancy**. There are a variety of different types of redundant phrases. As a society, we continue to remain unaware of many commonly used repetitive phrases. In fact, this paragraph is filled to capacity with them; there are six examples of redundancy. Finding them requires close scrutiny. Answers are inverted upside-down at the bottom of this page.

*The redundancies are: "combine two phrases or words together"; "variety of different types"; "continue to remain"; "filled to capacity"; "close scrutiny"; "inverted upside-down"*

# Yo momma is so **clairvoyant**, she says "bless you," and then people sneeze!

**clair·voy·ant** (clayr VOY unt)

adj. Able to predict the future accurately; able to perceive things beyond what people see naturally

n. Someone who possesses the ability described above

One meaning implies a broader extrasensory perception, not just an ability to predict things: **Clairvoyant** characters include those played by Patricia Arquette on *Medium* and Haley Joel Osment in *The Sixth Sense*, as well as Professor X of the X-Men. The other meaning refers more strictly to being able to foresee the future. ("You didn't have to be clairvoyant to predict Britney and K-Fed's marriage would fail.") Clairvoyant can also be a noun, meaning a clairvoyant person.

## Quizzle

Which powers below could be considered **clairvoyant**?

a) The power to predict the stock market by reading dryer lint filters

b) Warm ray vision (can gradually toast things)

c) The ability to predict infallibly the fourth-place horse in a race

d) The power to tell if people are hot just by listening to them on the phone

e) The ability to communicate with feta cheese

f) **Prehensile** (adapted for grasping) handle bar mustache

g) The ability to walk on the underside of water

h) The power to ungrind ground beef

*Answers: a,c,d*

**Yo momma** has such **gravitas**, the shadow of her butt weighs fifty pounds.

### grav·i·tas (GRAV i tahs)
n. An air of seriousness that commands respect

This is not an insult. If you have **gravitas**, you have weight, substance. In this sense, you can relate it to the word "gravity." Gravitas does not mean weight in a physical sense, however, so don't let our joke mislead you. Politicians and leaders need gravitas to convey to the public that they have the poise and wisdom to deal with serious problems. Nightly news anchors need gravitas. (Say that three times fast.) Comedians do not have gravitas. Nonetheless, Steven Colbert held a "gravitas-off" with Stone Phillips to see who could deliver the most **asinine** (see p. 77) lines with the most gravitas. Colbert will forever be remembered for his grave delivery of "When the smoke had cleared, both mugs were broken, and neither man could be truly called—World's Greatest Grandpa." For many reasons, "Gravitas" would be a bad name for a Mexican boy band. Though it does sound kind of like a Frito Lay snack.

**Yo Mnomma's Mnemonics:**

*"Gravitas - the corn chip for* **serious** *nacho fans!"*

**Yo momma** is so **ephemeral**, I can't even finish this joke!

### e·phem·er·al (uh FEM uhr uhl)
adj. Short-lived, lasting but a brief time

**Ephemeral** is there one minute and gone the next. These days, celebrity is ephemeral. Remember Spuds Mackenzie? Rico Suave? The joy of an author's childhood when these references actually existed…ah, so ephemeral. Ephemeral can also mean lasting only one day. In this case, morning dew is ephemeral.

# Yo momma's so **homely**, when she went to the beautician, it took 12 hours for a quote!

**home·ly** (HOHM lee)
adj. Unattractive, plain; unpretentious

This word can trip you up when you're reading, because you could think **homely** means making you feel at home ("homey"). In Britain, it actually does mean this, but then again they call trucks "lorries" and made Benny Hill a star. But fine, we'll suppress any **vestigial** (see p. 72) anti-redcoat sentiment and accept that homely can mean "suited for ordinary domestic life." Go from there to "not having elegance," and from there to "lacking physical attractiveness." The latter is its most common usage, and for some reason, many dictionaries use the example "a homely child." As if describing a child as unattractive is a normal thing to do. Who does that? It would be far more civil to lie and say the child is quite **comely**. What a difference a letter makes: Realty shows vs. reality shows; punk rock vs pun rock; and homely vs comely. Take out the "h" from homely and add a "c" and you have its **antithesis** (see p. 140), or direct opposite. Comely means attractive, fair.

## Quizzle

**Match the homely rock stars with their comely wives/exes.**

| | |
|---|---|
| • Rod Stewart | • Jerry Hall |
| • Seal | • Rachel Hunter |
| • Kid Rock | • Christie Brinkley |
| • Lyle Lovett | • Coco |
| • Billy Joel | • Heidi Klum |
| • Mick Jagger | • Julia Roberts |
| • Ice-T | • Pamela Anderson |

*Answers: Rod Stewart & Rachel Hunter; Seal & Heidi Klum; Kid Rock & Pamela Anderson; Lyle Lovett & Julia Roberts; Billy Joel & Christie Brinkley; Mick Jagger & Jerry Hall; Ice-T & Coco*

# Yo momma's so **antediluvian**, she knew
Cap'n Crunch while he was still a private.

**an·te·di·lu·vi·an** (an tih duh LOO vee uhn)
adj. From the time before the Biblical flood; old, outdated

**Antediluvian** comes from two Latin words that mean "before" and "flood." Not just any flood—the 40 days and 40 nights flood in the Bible. So from this etymology, its current more general meaning of being simply old or **antiquated** (outdated) makes sense. (And its great potential for yo momma-type insults becomes apparent.) We could say that Morten Andersen, nearly 50 and still kicking field goals in the NFL, is an antediluvian player. Jack Nicholson is something of an antediluvian actor, at least in creepily persistent get-the-girl roles. It can also be used as a noun—that is, we could say simply, "yo momma's an antediluvian."

# Yo momma's so **timorous**, she called 911
during *Scary Movie.*

**tim·or·ous** (TIM uhr uhs)
adj. Unconfident, fearful; showing a lack of confidence or displaying fearfulness

If you're **timorous**, you're scared. It doesn't necessarily apply only in instances like yo momma's, whose **timorousness** in the above example might border on paranoia. It can be used also to indicate a lack of social confidence. Asking someone out on a date might be a situation infused with a lot of timorous half-remarks and pointless questions. (Pay close attention to the usage in the preceding sentence. Timorous doesn't have to describe a person: Gestures or expressions that indicate a fearful disposition can also be called timorous.) If you're playing cards and make a timorous bet—with shaky hands and a tiny squeak of a voice— the other players will peg you as a timorous player.

# Yo momma's so prone to **hyperbole**,
### we hired her to write these jokes!

**hy·per·bo·le** (high PUR buh lee)
n. A figure of speech in which exaggeration is used for emphasis or effect

**Hyperbole** is exaggeration. Obvious and intentional exaggeration. All yo momma jokes are **hyperbolic**. Yo momma did not literally fall in love and break it. Nor is her belt size literally "equator." If it were, she would be a celestial body with her own orbiting moons, which would have a disastrous effect on the world's tides and rotation, so we'd know about it by now. These insults use hyperbole for comedic effect. The prefix "hyper-" comes from the Greek, meaning "over" or "beyond." Think hyperactive, hyper-spaz, hyperdrive.

# Yo momma's so **senescent**, somebody told
### her to act her age, and she died.

**se·nes·cent** (si NES uhnt)
adj. Growing old; aging

Things that are **senescent** are getting old. A rusty car on cinder blocks in somebody's front yard is senescent. Unsold fries at McDonald's that must be tossed are senescent. If you tell a joke a third time, looking for an extra laugh, your humor is senescent. When it's almost morning, the night is senescent. It's important to note from the preceding examples that not only people can be described as senescent. If we wrote any more, this example would enter the realm of **senescence**.

**Sampling:**
*Many a Menudo member's career was ended by inevitable senescence.*

# A **Question** for **Yo Momma**

An **interrogative** statement is one that asks or expresses a question. "Interrogative" can also be used as a noun to mean a sentence that asks a question. On *Jeopardy!*, contestants are forced to answer in interrogatives. They typically say, "Who is _____?" or "What is _____?" Though, technically, one could use alternative interrogative phrases.

**Alternative interrogative responses on *Jeopardy!*:**

*"This Florida state capital is home to Florida State University."*

- How 'bout a little bit of Tallahassee?

- Who's your Tallahassee?

- Am I just bubbling over with ecstasy as I answer "Tallahassee" or what?

- If I said "Tallahassee," would you love me forever?

- You want me to say "Tallahassee," don't you?

- Qué es Tallahassee?

Fill in the blanks with the word that best disses yo momma.

**1. Yo momma's** so _____, Bigfoot takes *her* picture.

   a) timorous

   b) hirsute

   c) depilated

   d) all of the above

**2. Yo momma's** so _____, she puts mayo on aspirin!

   a) voracious

   b) rapacious

   c) ravenous

   d) all of the above

**3. Yo momma's** breath is so _____, people on the PHONE hang up!

   a) agnostic

   b) fetid

   c) atavistic

   d) meltorned

**4. Yo momma's** skin is so _____, she makes Casper look **swarthy** (of dark complexion).

   a) jaundiced

   b) fetid

   c) pallid

   d) anti-rheinhold

*If you need to review a word for this or any quiz, look in the index (p. 161), where you'll find a complete list of words along with their corresponding page numbers.*

*Answers: 1b; 2d; 3b; 4c*

## Words That Didn't Make It Into The Dictionary

The idea of learning new words is to learn new ideas. These new ideas, in turn, help you express more complex and specific ideas in fewer words. Instead of having to say yo momma is "a vicious old hag who is prone to wandering a lot," you can say yo momma is "a **peripatetic harridan**" (see p. 79 and p. 52). You can more clearly express your ideas and feelings. And get chicks. Everyone knows the ladies love it when you express your ideas and feelings clearly.

Every year a team of linguists chooses new words (**neologisms:** nee AHL uh jizms) to admit into the dictionary. Every year some don't make it: Sometimes words just aren't necessary. Enjoy these words that didn't make it in.

- **pleln** – The area between your arm and front yard

- **sampleton** – The person in the picture that comes with a wallet

- **fruttle** – Clown feces

- **ploof** – To lose a contact lens in a urinal

- **meltorn** – To begin gradually to resemble Phil Donahue

- **crench** – To lean against the sink and get your crotch wet

- **chorkan** – The act of leaving Reston, Virginia, to commit a chorkan ("I chorkanned yesterday," said Roger as he put his pants back on)

- **phib** – To claim you're awake when somebody calls, even though you've been sleeping

- **deodritus** – The last remaining flakes of deodorant scraped onto your armpit

- **leonamania** – A morbid obsession with Ponce de León

# Yo momma is so laconic.

**la·con·ic** (luh KON ik)
adj.  See below

**Laconic** describes a person, piece of writing, etc., that conveys much by saying little.


# Yo momma's so oblivious, she thought "bling-bling" was a panda.

**ob·liv·i·ous** (uhb LIV ee uhs)
adj.  Totally unaware of what's happening

In the above example, yo momma is **oblivious** to contemporary culture.  Teenagers always think their parents are oblivious to everything, and then, years later, realize that maybe they had it backward.  A man can be oblivious to the feelings a woman might have for him, not noticing her little acts of flirtation.  Until recently, America was largely oblivious to growing resentment in the Middle East.

## What Should Be The Word Origin But Isn't:

**Oblivion** is the noun form. It can mean both "the state of being oblivious" (the oblivion of a coma) or "the state of being forgotten," as in: "Former sitcom child stars have a tough time adjusting from fame to living in oblivion."  There should have been an old Greek myth wherein all those who lost value in society went to a magical land called Oblivion.  They hatched a plan together to become relevant to society and make their return, only to realize that they had come to love their State of Oblivion more than the old society with all its trappings.  That's not the word origin, but it should be.

**Yo momma** is so **succulent**, she creates her own au jus when she sleeps!

**suc·cu·lent** (SUK yoo lent)
adj. Juicy and tender

Perhaps it's more dangerous to utter yo momma compliments than insults. One does not like to think of a mother as "succulent." Unless that "one" is Oedipus. **Succulent** means "juicy," though we have yet to see a pair of low-riding sweat pants with the word "succulent" across the butt. Give it time. More generally, succulent can mean **delectable**, rich in desirable qualities. Meats are often described as succulent, which is another reason that you want to be careful to whose momma you attribute **succulence**.

**Yo momma's** voice is so **mellifluous**, she opens her mouth and wars stop!

**mel·lif·lu·ous** (muh LIF loo uhs)
adj. Pleasing to the ear, flowing with sweetness

**Mellifluous** sounds like what it means: There is a certain amount of **onomatopoeia** (see p. 99) to it. Mellifluous is pleasing to say and hear. The word flows sweetly off the tongue, much like the mellifluous tones of The Mormon Tabernacle Choir. In *Lord of the Rings*, Elven singing is magically mellifluous. Rosanne Barr's rendition of the *Star Spangled Banner* was not mellifluous, but rather **shrill** or **strident** (harsh, unpleasant).

---

### Word to Your Mother!

As you can see, the snaps above are not disses, but rather compliments. They are **laudatory** snaps. Laudatory means "complimentary, expressing praise," so "laudatory snaps" is somewhat contradictory, or an **oxymoron** (see p 107).

**Yo monotheistic momma's** Oscar speech:

"I'd like to thank God for giving me the strength to work hard to get where I am…"

**Monotheism** is the belief in one God. "Mono" means one and "theism" has to do with God. Judeo-Christian religions are monotheistic.

(mahn oh thee ISS tik); (mahn oh THEE izm)

**Yo polytheistic momma's** Oscar speech:

"I'd like to thank Demeter for the bountiful harvest and Hephaestus, without whom we would not have the cutlery to consume the harvest. I'd like to thank Zeus, of course, and oh… Athena for providing the wisdom."

Yo momma never got to thank her agent, because she was still thanking gods when the exit music started playing. We could break down **polytheism** for you—"poly" and "theistic," but we don't want to insult you. You get it: "believing in many gods."

(pahl ee thee ISS tik); (pahl ee THEE izm)

**Yo agnostic momma's** Oscar speech:

"I'd like to thank God, if he exists, for giving me strength. I could not have done this without him, unless, of course, there is no such thing, in which case…"

An **agnostic** is someone who isn't sure whether or not there is a God and, usually, someone who thinks it is impossible to know for sure. It can be a noun or an adjective.

(ag NOSS tik)

# Yo momma's victory was so **Pyrrhic**,
### we celebrated it at her funeral!

**Pyr·rhic** (PEER ik)

There are a few definitions for the word Pyrrhic:

1) In poetry, having two brief or unaccented syllables BORING!

2) Relating to an Ancient Greek dance ("Pyrrhic dance movements") SNOOZER!

3) Resembling Pyrrhus, who, on his way to defeating the Romans, sustained staggering losses in battles ("a Pyrrhic victory") AHHH... INTERESTING. AND USEFUL.

A **Pyrrhic** victory is so costly to the victor it can hardly be called a victory. If the Washington Redskins win a game, but all their star players get hurt and miss the playoffs, that's a Pyrrhic victory. If you're playing Risk or Stratego and you win, but you only have a few pieces left on the board, you've achieved a Pyrrhic victory. If you watch one TV on top of another broken TV, you have not had a Pyrrhic victory, but you just might be a redneck. The casualties sustained in a Pyrrhic victory are not restricted to lives lost, but also can refer to things like a loss of credibility or increased dissension in the ranks.

## *Word to Your Mother!*

Pyrrhic is a killer word to spell; it's been the bane of many a socially maladjusted spelling bee contestant. Our advice: Only use it when you have the insurance of a spell-check or really commit its spelling to memory.

# Yo momma's so **vociferous**, she melted her braces!

**vo·cif·er·ous** (vuh SIF uhr uhs) or (voh SIF uhr uhs)
adj. Loud and forceful

**Vociferous** people emit a constant and loud stream of noise. It's not necessarily informative talk, but it's constant and overpowering. Bobby Knight, one of the winningest college basketball coaches in history, talks to referees **vociferously**. That is, he yells at them, often in the form of many loud curses, one after another. The Hollywood image of military drill sergeants is one of demanding **vociferousness**, constantly berating soldiers and intimidating them by shouting insults.

A quick example to distinguish vociferous from **garrulous**: If yo momma hangs out with her friends and they don't get a word in edgewise because yo momma

> a) talks and talks about a range of meaningless, probably unrelated and perhaps foolish things, from goldfish to upholstery to the time she visited Oklahoma—yo momma is garrulous.

> b) talks and talks about how her friend needs to CHANGE HER HAIR RIGHT NOW because it currently MAKES HER LOOK LIKE DEE SNYDER and she should also JOIN HER GYM because her Pilates instructor will stop her from looking like GRIMACE FROM MCDONALD'S, and on and on—yo momma is vociferous.

And a final point: No matter whether yo momma is vociferous or garrulous, if she's either, she's **loquacious**, which means simply that yo momma talks a lot.

# I schooled **yo momma** so much, she's **erudite**!

**er·u·dite** (AIR yoo dight)
adj. Having or showing profound knowledge

If you're **erudite**, you are highly educated. Your house is wallpapered with graduate degrees. Professors are erudite, and might while away their time writing erudite criticisms of erudite commentaries about erudite books (that nobody ever reads). A yo momma combatant's street smarts represent a different sort of **erudition**. The word "erudite" sounds a little pretentious, so it can impart a little bit of snobbishness to the intelligence it describes.

**Words not to put in front of your name if you're a boxer, or worst Smurf names:**

- Erudite

- **Mawkish** (see p. 84)

- Bipolar

- Adhesive

- Obsessive-Compulsive

- Bulimic

- **Taciturn** (see p. 50)

- Self-Aggrandizing

- Passive-Aggressive

- **Amorphous** (see p. 50)

- Narcoleptic

- Festering

- **Turgid** (see p. 54)

# Yo momma's skin's so **jaundiced**, she sweats butter!

**jaun·diced** (JAWN dissed) or (JAHN dissed)
adj. Having yellowish skin, as if diseased; having an outlook distorted by bitterness or resentment

We're not sure how they got from grotesque yellow skin to the second, more psychological meaning. But if you were to pick a color that represents the sort of embittered, envious, prejudiced, world-weary viewpoint that is **jaundiced**, sickly yellow is as good as any. Critics write jaundiced reviews of Adam Sandler movies, perhaps because they never achieved the same success from that screenplay about a hard-nosed cop partnered with a wily cockatoo. Decades of being a soap opera actress surprisingly haven't left Susan Lucci jaundiced; even as younger actresses beat her out for awards, she remains upbeat and supportive of others. Jaundice is a bad name for your child, an awful paint color, and an even worse band name. You don't want jaundiced skin and you don't want a jaundiced outlook on life.


# Yo momma's so dirty, you can tell her age by the **concentric** rings underneath her armpits.

**con·cen·tric** (kuhn SEN trik)
adj. Having a common center (as with circles)

The rings in a tree trunk are **concentric**: They share the same center. They get bigger as they go outward. An archery target's rings are concentric. When you toss a rock in the water, the water ripples out in concentric circular waves. And yo momma, we're sorry to say, is so **corpulent** (see p. 4), people revolve around her in concentric orbits.

## 19th Century Japanese
## Yo Momma Haiku Battle

**Yo momma** expands
Filling air like morning fog;
Infinite fat one

**Yo momma** very
Old like roots of Mt. Fuji
Stretching, forgotten

Fruits and nectars both
Elude her desperate grasp
So poor, **Yo momma**

Clouds fear **Yo momma**
Pocked face of a vulture-pecked
Carcass, so ugly.

**Maternal wonder**
More rolls than sushi combo
Awake from slumber

*The challenge of Haiku is to be* **laconic** *(see p. 24), or to say a lot in a little. If you want to attempt some advanced yo momma slams, the syllable pattern above is five for the first line, seven for the second, and five for the third.*

**Yo momma's** so fat, she has to iron her pants on the driveway. She's the **leviathan** of mommas.

**le·vi·a·than** (luh VYE uh thun)
n. Something unusually large; the largest or most massive thing of its kind

The word **leviathan** comes from the Bible. It was the name for a massive sea monster, hence a common use of the word to mean a ship or whale. Leviathan came to mean anything huge, or, more specifically and uniquely, "the biggest of its kind," as in "Andre the Giant was the leviathan of professional wrestlers"; "Devo was the leviathan of one-hit wonders"; or "that Great Dane created the leviathan of canine bowel movements." A synonym is "**behemoth**," also a biblical term that described a large sea creature (maybe a hippo). Clearly, in biblical times, people were more preoccupied with large sea creatures than we are today.

## Quizzle

**Which one of these words really came from the Bible?**

- Jezebel (1 Kings 16:31)

- Martinet (John 1:12)

- Fudgecicle (Exodus 3:19)

*Answer:*
*The word "Jezebel" comes from Jezebel, the cruel and evil biblical queen of Israel who tried to kill numerous prophets. Thus, the word means "a wicked, scheming woman." **Martinet** (see p. 123) means "a strict disciplinarian" and comes from a French general, Jean Martinet. Fudgecicle did not really come from the Bible. It is, however, a portmanteau word (see p. 11).*

**Yo momma's** feet are so **callous**, when she
    walks on a wooden floor, it sounds like she's
    tap dancing.

> **cal·lous**  CAL luhs ("CAL" sounds like the beginning
> of "California")
>> adj.  Having or exhibiting a lack of care; covered
>> with calluses

If something is **callous**, it's hardened.  It can mean literally
having calluses (hardened parts of the skin), as in the above
example (and, yes, the spellings are different), and can also mean
"emotionally hardened or toughened, unfeeling."  While you can
have a callous sole, you can also have a callous soul.  When Eric
and Lyle Menendez, the Beverly Hills convicted murderers,
bought Rolex watches between their parents' murders and their
funeral, this was a callous gesture.

**Yo momma's** so ugly and lazy, she has the
    perfect **sinecure**:  She's a scarecrow.

> **si·ne·cure**  (SYE nuh kyoor)
>> n.  A job that requires no effort but provides the worker
>> ample money or status

The word **sinecure** comes from Latin words that mean,
literally, "without care."  William Hung, the cringe-inducing
singer on *American Idol*, now makes big bucks playing to big
crowds while singing bad karaoke.  Quite the sinecure.  Paris
Hilton received millions for "acting" like a snob. She had a
manicure, a pedicure, and a sinecure.  Other examples of
sinecures:  corporate board memberships, managing one's own
massive inheritance, being a political appointee (in some cases).
Writing yo momma jokes spotlighting **esoteric** (see p. 142)
words?  Definitely.

# Yo momma's so full of **innuendo**—if y'know what I mean!

**inn·u·en·do** (in you EN doh)
n. A backhanded, inexplicit remark about somebody or something, usually of a mocking or suggestive nature

Let's just say yo momma doesn't just sit AROUND the house, she sits AROUND the BLOCK. An **innuendo** is an indirect or subtle, usually derogatory implication in expression. It's an insinuation. In other words, an innuendo hints at something. An innuendo doesn't have to be derogatory, however. Innuendos are often used to describe something that hints at the **salacious** (lustful, indecent) without actually spelling it out. "Why don't I slip into something a little more comfortable?" can be considered an innuendo.

Masters of this sort of innuendo include Shakespeare ("making the beast with two backs") and the creators of *Three's Company* (the *Macbeth* of its time), who created innuendo through the use of **double entendre** (ahn TAHN druh). A double entendre is a figure of speech that can be understood literally, but can also be interpreted to have another often more risqué meaning. *Three's Company* characters practically spoke in double entendre, whether they were hanging shower curtains, picking locks, or baking casseroles. Innuendo can, but does not have to use double entendre.

**10 expressions that sound like double entendres, but aren't:**

- "Dimming the lights"
- "The march of the penguins"
- "TiVo-ing Martha Stewart"
- "Appreciating Burgess Meredith"
- "Summarizing your portfolio"
- "Extrapolating pi"
- "Ordering a mocha latte"
- "Fudging your golf score"
- "Defrosting the icebox"
- "Smelling your Sharpie"

**Yo momma's** reasoning is so **specious**,
she was fired from an M&M factory for throwing
out the W's!

**spe·cious** (SPEE shuhs)
adj. Plausible on the surface, but actually wrong

From the above yo momma joke, you could deduce that **specious**
means "stupid." You could also reasonably think that it means
"backward" or "seen from a different perspective." All would be
perfectly reasonable, but specious, definitions of the word. Specious
means "seemingly correct on the surface, but, when you get down to
it, not correct at all." You most commonly see the phrases "specious
reasoning" or a "specious argument." And though it may seem like
a specious stretch, specious can also mean "deceptively attractive"—
nice from far, but far from nice.

### *Specious Facts (facts that sound like they might be true but aren't)*

- The reason firemen slide down poles is to wipe their pants
  free of flammable crumbs that might have accrued at lunch.

- Soccer was invented on pirate ships as a means of cleaning
  the deck.

- Women originally wore makeup for warmth.

- The dishwasher was invented by accident.

- In Belgium, it is considered an insult to stand up.

- A Navajo tribe communicates in a silent language that
  consists of rapid weight loss and weight gain.

- The letter "w" was added to the English language in 1954.

- Cheech and Chong borrowed the plots of their movies from
  Arthur Miller plays.

- Dr. Phil grew his mustache to help with his allergies.

- The bagpipe was originally made from human lung.

- Until 1964, people did not pour milk in their cereal—they
  poured ranch dressing.

## Specious Facts (cont'd)

- A small amount of crystal meth is used in the manufacturing of Cool Ranch Doritos.

- Lyndon Johnson had a tattoo of a cantaloupe on his hip.

- In 1938, "Milt" was the most popular name for both men and women.

- The washing machine was invented before the washboard.

- The U.S. national anthem actually has three verses, but everyone just knows the first. The second and third verses concern oatmeal and pipe cleaners, respectively.

- The country of Trinidad and Tobago was originally called Trinidad and/or Tobago.

- In Uzbekistan, all food is consumed in gaseous form.

- In a lifetime, a typist's fingers will travel 8 million light years.

- Life Savers have holes because they were originally used as fish bait.

- George Washington Carver killed himself with a peanut.

- The most constipated animal in the world is the polar bear.

- The check mark was originally a letter in the alphabet.

- The kings in a deck of cards represent the members of Bachman Turner Overdrive.

- The reason John Hancock signed his name so large was that he had hands twice the size of a normal human being.

- Alfred Hitchcock did not keep a wallet. Rather, he kept all of his money in his mouth.

Are these really specious facts? Or do these facts become more **asinine** (see p. 77) than specious? Did we just demonstrate speciousness in our claim that the facts above were specious?

# Yo momma's so **reprobate**, when she got called to jury duty, SHE was found guilty.

**rep·ro·bate** (REP ruh bate)
n. One who is immoral or unethical
adj. Immoral, unethical, unprincipled

**Reprobate** means "morally unprincipled" as an adjective, "a morally unprincipled person" as a noun, and "to abandon to damnation" as a verb. Your reprobate momma plays moral limbo; how low can she go? She steals from Salvation Army donation jars. She prank calls orphans pretending she's going to adopt them. She beats baby seals… with panda cubs. Reprobate is a pretty bad thing to call someone. It can mean "rejected by God and beyond hope of salvation," and that's tough to twist into a compliment.

### "Scruples for Reprobates" or "Immoral Dilemmas"

The moral code for reprobates is a bit loose. See below for some ethical dilemmas that might go through a reprobate's mind.

*You're driving at night and hit a dog, possibly killing it. You see it has a collar with a tag. No one witnesses the accident. Do you broil or bake the dog?*

*The only available spot in the parking lot is reserved for the handicapped. You are in a hurry and won't be very long. After you park there, do you key the car next to you for fun?*

*You e-mail your picture to a gorgeous person you met on the Internet. You've gained 30 pounds since the picture was taken. Do you make your date pay for the two ham sandwiches you consume during your dinner, or just skip out on the check?*

**Yo momma's** skin is so **lucid**, she models for circulatory system diagrams. Aw yeah!

**lu·cid** (LOO sid)
    adj. Transparent; easy to understand (can refer to a person or a thing); bright

**Lucid** means clear, both in physical terms and as in "easily understood." We try to write these explanations **lucidly**, so you can understand them. Via pop culture references, we **elucidate** (shed light on, make clear) a word's meaning and usage for people who learn from TV and the Internet. Lucid can also mean clear-headed, mentally sound: Ozzy Osbourne's only lucid moments seem to occur when he sings. Lawyers sometimes avoid **lucidity** on purpose.

**Sampling:**

*When the driver explained he had swerved to "avoid the dragon," the officer suspected his mental state was not entirely* **lucid**.

**Yo momma's** dresses are so **diaphanous**, people crawl under her to avoid mosquitoes.

**di·aph·a·nous** (dye AFF uhn us)
    adj. Gauzily see-through and delicate, usually applying to fabric

Wow, that's a tough word to use in a yo momma joke. If you can see through something and it's light and delicate, it's **diaphanous**. Mosquito nets are diaphanous—you can see through them, but the mesh is tight enough to obscure things slightly. There's a lot of diaphanous fabric worn on the red carpet at events like the Oscars so stars can be tastefully provocative. **Lucid** fabrics, by contrast, would cross that line. There's a haziness to things that are diaphanous, something gauzy and dreamy about them. It's also kind of a cool thing to name a child: Diaphanous.

# Yo momma's so **impassive**, she makes Spock look **effusive**!

**im·pas·sive** (im PASS iv)
adj.  Unaffected by or not showing emotion

If you're **impassive**, you don't show emotion.  You hear news of a family death and you react as if you didn't hear anything newsworthy.  Jon Mark Karr, who claimed to have murdered child model JonBenét Ramsey, maintained the impassive demeanor that we associate with unrepentant, amoral killers throughout the short time it took to reveal that he had nothing to do with the child's death, thus, exposing him as a **mountebank** (see p. 126).  Golf announcers speak in hushed impassive tones.  Sometimes when hip-hop artists try to act, they paste on largely impassive tough-guy expressions and trudge through two hours of script, often with predictably bad results (see 50 Cent in *Get Rich or Die Tryin'*).

**ef·fus·ive** (if FYOO siv)
adj.  Gushing with emotion

Excessive emotional outpourings can be described as **effusive**.  An effusive reaction to winning a game of Monopoly might be performing a protracted, overly elaborate victory dance around the board, waving sparklers and singing "We Are the Champions."  The NFL has banned effusive touchdown celebrations, presumably thinking fans will better enjoy impassive reactions.  Nothing like an understated, stoic acceptance of a touchdown to get the fans pumped up!  Though effusive, which usually is used in front of words like "praise," "greeting," and "welcome," can document a genuine overflow of emotion ("After we helped him douse the gasoline fire on his chest, he thanked us **effusively**"), a possible implication of the word is insincerity.  Take Kelly Ripa, the bubbly co-host of *Live with Regis and Kelly*.  Ripa's **effusiveness** is so over the top that, periodically, it smacks of insincerity.  Same goes for Joan Rivers, praising celebrities' outfits on the red carpet before the Academy Awards.

# **Yo momma's** so **diminutive**, she uses ChapStick for deodorant.

**di·min·u·tive** (di MIN yoo tihv)
adj. Unusually small, tiny

People often remark on the **diminutiveness** of actors when they encounter them in real life. You've heard that the camera adds ten pounds; it also adds several inches (or, at least, editing and careful angles do). You might not know, for instance, Tom Cruise and Sylvester Stallone are both under 5'8" tall, and that Johnny Depp is less than five feet. OK, maybe that last one's **hyperbole** (see p. 20). iPods are getting more diminutive with each generation. When will the fingernail implantiPods arrive? Or the umbiliPods?

# **Yo momma's** like the Energizer bunny: **indefatigable**!

**in·de·fat·i·ga·ble** (in di FAT ig uh buhl)
adj. Untiring in one's persistence

Aw, snap! Actually, this isn't an insult. It just means that yo momma's tireless. It doesn't specify, however, what she does so tirelessly. If she were an **indefatigable** nag, never tiring of telling you to do your homework and take out the trash, that would be one thing. Think "cannot be fatigued." OK, you can stop thinking that now. Marathoners are indefatigable runners. A lot of C.E.O.'s get to the top with an indefatigable work ethic. You may ask, why not just use the word "tireless"? Yeah, why not use tireless? You know what, forget this word. Let us never speak of this again!

# Yo momma is so **masochistic**, she wrote this joke herself!

**m a s·o c h·i s·t i c** (mass uh KISS tik)
adj. Deriving pleasure or gratification from being abused by oneself or others

**Masochism** (MASS uh kizm) is another **eponym** (see p. 62). It comes from the Austrian writer Leopold Ritter von Sacher-Masoch, whose love for abuse apparently stemmed from his parents giving him an insufferably long name. Masoch wrote a novel you'll never read that features a character who asks a woman to treat him in increasingly degrading ways. We've all made some bad decisions in our lives that make us seem like masochists. **Masochistic** behavior, or **masochism**, can refer to physical self-abuse (like cutting oneself) or psycholgocial self-abuse, such as staying in an unhealthy relationship, attending law school, or watching *E!*.

## A Masochist's Day Planner

8:00 Wake up, hold hand in waffle maker.
8:30 Get dressed in T-shirt that reads "You are with stupid."
9:00 Duct-tape eyelids, have every cosmetics employee at Macy's spray face with newest fragrance.
11:30 Repeatedly hole-punch arm.
1:00 Have left eye melon-balled out by Leonard.
1:30 File abrasions into skin, bathe in red pepper.
2:30 Advanced Sudoku.
4:00 Loathe self.
5:00 Get painful tattoo.
6:00 Remove tattoo with painful laser procedure.
7:00 Affix fish hook to lip, have someone reel hook in.
8:00 MTV: *Real World/Road Rules Challenge*.
9:00 Thumb in vice, power drill foot, "get organized."
10:00 Take a deep breath, then watch *Waiting to Exhale*. Don't resume breathing 'til the end.
12:00 Bed (either hot coals, nails, or rabid geese).

# The Baker's Dozens

**Yo momma** is such an awful **patissier**
(pah tis YAY) **(pastry chef)** that her
gingerbread house was condemned!

**Yo momma** is such a bad **sommelier**
(suh mul YAY) **(wine steward)** there's so
much cork in her pour, you can tack a picture in it!

**Yo momma** is such a terrible
**poissonier** (pwa sohn YAY) **(fish station
cook)** that the only thing she prepares is crappie!

**Yo momma** is such a bad **garde-manger**
(gard mon ZHAY) **(cold food chef)** that her
gazpacho burned my mouth!

**Yo momma** is such a bad **boulanger**
(boo lahn ZHAY) **(bread maker)** that her
sourdough is sweet!

The words above are of little use to laymen. However,
as evidenced in previous snaps, yo momma is likely a
**gourmand** (goor MAHND), which means that she is a
lover of food and/or eats in excess. If yo momma is a
**gourmet** (goor MAY), on the other hand, she is more
refined in her tastes. Yo gourmet momma wants the
Grey Poupon, while yo gourmand momma wants the
Poupon, the French's, and the ketchup for the 45 hot
dogs she is about to consume.

# No Wrong Answers

In your opinion, who is the worst supervillain?

- Dr. Loquacious
- The Procrastinator
- Jaundice
- Succulent Man

In your opinion, what's the best name for a rapper using our phonetic spellings? (It worked for Ludacris.)

- Uhfemuhruhl (Ephemeral)
- Yoobikwituhs (Ubiquitous)
- Repruhbate (Reprobate)
- Igreejuhs (Egregious)

In your opinion, which character makes the best Microsoft Word help icon?

- The Indefatigable Hare Krishna
- The Effusive Caveman
- The Erudite Sumo Wrestler
- The Timorous Half-Orc

# Yo momma's so **amorphous**, when she fills a void, she FILLS a void!

### a·mor·phous (uh MOHR fuss)
adj. Shapeless; vague; lacking focus

Something that is **amorphous** is shapeless. The Blob, from the cult classic film starring Steve McQueen, is amorphous. Amoebas, which constantly shift shape, are amorphous. Cloud masses can be amorphous. Amorphous things have no pattern or structure or constancy. An incoherent, unclear, **meandering** (winding like an old stream) argument can be called amorphous. If someone has an amorphous personality, you can't quite pin it down.

### Sampling:

*The* **amorphous** *grey ooze enveloped the dwarven mage as the paladin attempted to cast a fireball spell, and the troll king Gorgorath swung his +5 vorpal sword across the chain-mailed chest of the young elf thief, Zeldenar, whose ring of protection (armor class -5) cast an aura of light about them, blinding the menacing umberhulk guardians, whose gaze caused 4-8 hit points of damage per melee round—we mean, uh, if you're, like, into that kind of thing.*

# Yo momma is so **perfunctory** (insert recycled yo momma joke here).

### per·func·tor·y (puhr FUNGK tuhr ee)
adj. Done with no effort or thought

All right, we need to fill a second word for this page. **Perfunctory's** as good a word as any. Throw down a definition, maybe a little joke, pop culture reference, a little self-reference… fine, good, we're done. This entire entry has been written in a perfunctory manner, performed merely as a routine duty, hastily and **superficially** (in a shallow way).

**Yo momma's** belly button is so **abysmal**,
it's got an echo!

**a·bys·mal** (uh BIZ muhl)
adj. Terrible, extremely bad; very deep

Once again, let's start with the physical. **Abysmal** is related to "abyss" (a canyon), so abysmal means immeasurably deep. Something that stretches limitlessly downward could reasonably be thought of as "immeasurably bad," which is what abysmal is most often used to mean. In this sense, it is similar to **egregious** (see p. 7). If your school's basketball team goes winless, it had an abysmal season. In your life, you might, and you will, encounter abysmal ignorance, abysmal manners, and—how 'bout this **oxymoron** (see p. 107)—abysmal shallowness (such as that displayed by the characters on the show *Laguna Beach*).

**Yo momma's** so **solipsistic**,
she married herself!

**sol·ip·sis·tic** (sah lip SIS tik)
adj. Believing only oneself exists; highly self-centered

**Solipsism** is the theory that the self is the only thing that exists. It's a philosophical word that, for obvious reasons, can also be used to describe a general preoccupation with oneself (**egocentrism**). **Solipsism** is an idea that every college sophomore thinks he is the first to think of, until he later learns that so many other people have thought of it, there's a word for it and everything. This mentality, the "I know everything when you really don't" mindset, can be described by using the word "**sophomoric**," which is derived from the Greek loosely meaning "wise fool."

# **Yo momma's** so **ostentatious**, she makes Mr. T look understated!

**os·ten·ta·tious** (ahs ten TAY shuhs)
adj.  Flashy, intended to impress others

**Ostentatious** means showy.  If something is ostentatious, it's meant to attract the attention of others and to impress them.  It's an insult to call something or someone ostentatious, and, yet, in today's hip hop culture, as with many things, that which was once looked down upon is celebrated.  *MTV Cribs* checks out young stars' homes, searching for the world's most ostentatious absurdities: solid gold stripper poles, giant shrubberies in the shapes of their owners, cars with TVs everywhere, including the rims.  All the while, MTV uses ostentatious editing to create the illusion of content.  The show *My Super Sweet 16* features **vacuous** (see p. 79) parents who spoil their obnoxious children by throwing them preposterously ostentatious birthday parties.

**Ostentatious displays for your sweet 16 party:**

- A cake shaped like you holding another cake
- A unitard made entirely of diamond
- Your name monogrammed in professional calligraphy on every blade of grass in your yard
- Solid gold teeth, ears, and eyes
- A mink-framed Rembrandt held at eye-level by the World's Stillest Man
- An entrance that features you riding in on endangered pandas
- A round of "Happy Birthday" performed live by Clay Aiken (verses 2 and 3 included)
- Stuntman "human candles" on your cake
- A "personal listener" to whom all inquiries must be addressed
- Invitations handed out by the cast of *According to Jim*

# Yo Momma Through History

## Colonial

**Yo momma's** head is so big, she needs a
*four*-cornered hat!

## Amish

**Ye mother** is so un-humble that she wore an
off white bonnet to the barn raising.

## The Dark Ages

**Ye mum** is so ravenous that the town barber uses
her as a leech during his bloodlettings!

## Shakespearian

**Thou matriarch** is by no means valiant; For she
dost fear the soft and tender fork of a poor worm.
Hie she to a nunnery!

## The Future

*INITIALIZING INSULT*: The cloning unit which
resulted in **yo momma's** creation is defective.
The defect has been identified as an excess of body
weight. *END INSULT*.

# Yo momma's such a **parasite**, when she wants to watch TV, she goes to Best Buy!

**par·a·site** (PAIR uh syte)
  n. Someone who, without giving anything back, benefits from others; a moocher

A **parasite** is a biological term that refers to an organism that lives on or in another organism. From this, the word has come to describe people who receive support from others and offer nothing in return. The 30-year-old man who still lives in Mom and Dad's basement and pays no rent is a parasite living off his parents. Are you a parasite to society? Do you pretend to be interested in free samples, "tasting" until you've eaten a full meal? What's the proper etiquette when you taste the free sample and decide to walk away? Do you try to close the loop in sales speak by saying something like "Hmmm... That's good pita wedge and artichoke dip. I'll consider this and come back if I'm interested in moving forward." Is that better than just nodding, raising eyebrows superficially, and, as they stare at you, simply walking away without uttering a word? Anyway, what were we talking about?

# Yo momma's so **saprophytic**, she has a compost mattress!

**sap·ro·phyt·ic** (sap ruh FIT ik)
  adj. Living on dead or decaying organic matter

Although "**saprophyte**" is, most accurately, another biological term that applies to various fungi, microorganisms, etc., it's fun to extend this meaning to apply to "May-December" relationships, or those between people whose age difference is relatively vast. Anna Nicole Smith, who married a rich guy 40 times her age, is a legendary saprophyte who lived off the **largesse** (see p. 6) of her sugar daddy while he was alive, and off the wealth she inherited after his death.

**Yo momma's** so **indigent**, when she was kicking a can down the street, I asked what she was doing, and she said "moving!"

**in·di·gent** (IN di juhnt)
adj. Extremely poor; lacking the necessities of life

That's just sad. If yo momma's sole possession is a can, that is. It doesn't even sound like there's anything in the can, or else she wouldn't be kicking it so haphazardly. Yo momma isn't just poor. She's **indigent**. Indigent means lacking even the basics: food, shelter, cable television.

**Yo momma's** so **gauche**, she ordered her sushi well done!

**gauche** (GOHSH)
adj. Unsophisticated, so much so as to make social situations difficult

**Gauche** people lack social grace and polish. Not surprisingly, this snooty, insulting word is of French origin. Picking your teeth with the corner of a sugar packet, while surprisingly effective (trust us), is gauche.

## What Should Be The Word Origin But Isn't:

During the French Revolution, the city of **Gauche**, France was a waystation for military troops. The troops would be quartered in noblemen's homes, where they would display hideous manners and a lack of refinement. Unfortunately for the townspeople, the city itself soon became associated with this lack of social propriety and "gauche" became a French (and later an English) word. Don't mention this story at a cocktail party or include it in an essay for history class; the entire story, including the city of Gauche, is made up: It's a fabrication. This is not the word origin—not even close—but it should be!

# **Your momma's** so **taciturn**, she makes Calvin Coolidge look like Rutherford B. Hayes! What up, yo!

**tac·i·turn** (TASS i turn)
adj. Inclined to be untalkative

OK, so you need a little history for this yo momma. Calvin Coolidge, unlike most of today's pundits and politicians, was quiet and reserved by nature. But Hayes? You couldn't shut him up with a doorstop. President Coolidge wasn't a talker, but not in the sense that George W. Bush is not a talker. Coolidge was not a **maladroit** (unskilled) speaker; he was simply **habitually** (as a matter of habit) reserved and uncommunicative. The root of this word is the Latin *tacitus*, meaning silent. (See **tacit**: Just look about a half-inch down.)

There you go. Tacit means "unspoken." But it's used often to mean "unspoken, but understood." There are tacit rules in society, tacit agreements we make with one another. When you're next to use the ATM, you have a tacit understanding to stand about four feet behind the current user. Know what's fun? Instead, stand six inches back, or 20 feet.

**Here are some other tacit rules in society and fun ways to break them:**

*Tacit rule:* In elevators, you stare at the numbers and stay quiet.
*How to break it*: As someone exits, just as the doors close, whisper "I love you...."

*Tacit rule:* At urinals, you keep to yourself.
*How to break it*: Be really friendly and talkative. Be **loquacious**, **garrulous**. Recite limericks.

*Tacit rule:* At the super market checkout, you put down the plastic grocery divider wand between your items and the items of the customer in front of you.
*How to break it*: Put an additional divider on the floor between yourself and the customer in front of you. Dare them to cross it.

# What Has Yo Momma Taught You So Far?

**1.** I sent her a "singing mammogram" is an example of a(n) _____.

   a) portmanteau

   b) mnemonic

   c) malapropism

   d) million dollar idea

**2.** Who are the most **ostentatious** dressers?

   a) priests

   b) pimps

   c) grandparents

   d) all of the above

**3.** Fill in the blanks with the correct word below.
If a child star has a _____ appetite, she is likely to become _____, which will cause her career to fade into _____, because shallow American society values only unrealistic, _____ body types.

Words: corpulent; emaciated; voracious; oblivion

**4.** Time to play everyone's favorite game:
**Diaphanous** or **Lucid**?

   a) your windshield

   b) your brand new clear plastic shower curtain

   c) your shower curtain when it starts to fog up with an uncertain disgusting film and partially disintegrates due to mold

   d) your aquarium full of water

   e) **undulating** (moving like waves) curtains in a perfume ad

*Answers: 1c; 2b; 3 voracious, corpulent, oblivion, emaciated; 4 a) lucid, b) lucid, c) diaphanous, d) diaphanous, e) diaphanous*

**Yo momma's** such a **harridan**, she walked into a haunted house and came out with a paycheck!

**har·ri·dan** (HAIR i dn)
n. A mean old woman

A **harridan** is a hag, a shrew. Yo momma, the harridan, scolds aggressively and won't lay off bossing people around. Her detractors sometimes refer to conservative political critic Ann Coulter, despite her still relatively young age, as a harridan. Its usage, some speculate, comes from a French term that meant "old horse." Incidentally, yo momma is synonymously a **virago** (rhymes with "Chicago") and **termagant** (has the same emphasis as "permanent"). Amazing how many words there are for ill-tempered, screaming women. Makes you wonder about linguists' wives.

**Yo momma** is so **epic**, when she steps on a scale, it says "To be continued!"

**ep·ic** (EP ik)
adj. Large-scale, heroic, grand in scale or scope

A person is not generally described as **epic**. The **pejorative** (see p. 140) element at work here is equating your momma to a work of literature that is extraordinary in size, length, or scale. Her girth is so impressive that minstrels will sing of it and pass it on in oral tradition. *Lord of the Rings* is both an epic film and an epic literary series. Homer wrote *The Iliad* and *The Odyssey*, both epic poems. The movies *Ishtar* and *Waterworld* were both epic failures—not just because they were long movies that failed, but also because they failed on such a grand scale.

**Yo momma** is such a seeker of
**schadenfreude**, she signed you up for
*American Idol!*

**scha·den·freu·de** (SHAHd n froyd uh)
n. Satisfaction or pleasure felt at someone else's misfortune

Leave it to the Germans to come up with this word. The
Eskimos have hundreds of words for snow (but evidently none
for **superfluous**—see p. 86), and the Germans have hundreds of
words for suffering. The word origin comes from *Schaden* (harm)
+ *Freude* (joy). Man, those Germans have a way of melding
words together. **Schadenfraude** is an awesome word which
you will find yourself using a lot more as you get older. You
experience schadenfreude when a friend who seemingly has it all
gets divorced and you feel a guilty pang of satisfaction, or when
you experience an odd joy watching the faces of losing Oscar
nominees when the winner is announced.

## Quizzle

**Which are real German words for various types of suffering?**

- **Weltschmerz** – The grief and painful melancholy one feels
  when observing the state of the world

- **Miksenshpice** – To be secretly ashamed over the lackluster
  appearance of one's MySpace profile page

- **Geisteskrank** – Literally, "of an ill mind"; describing
  someone suffering from mental illness

- **Schmenderikweit** – The agony one feels upon his battleship
  being sunk in the **eponymous** (see p. 62) game

- **Angst** – General anxiety and distress

- **Schauvenschtorp** – The disappointment one feels when
  flipping on a TV show and realizing it's the one episode
  you've already seen

*Answer: Weltschmerz, Geisteskrank, and Angst are real, but you probably knew that.*

# Yo mom is a palindrome!

Oh, no you di'n't! You di'n't just call my momma a palindrome! Actually, yo "momma" is not a palindrome. Yo "mom" is. Yo "dad" is, too.

> **pal·in·drome** (PAL in drohm)
> ("PAL" sounds like ol' buddy ol' pal...)
> n. A word or phrase spelled identically backward and forward

Examples of **palindromes** are "race car," "radar," and "kayak." Names that are palindromes include Bob, Anna, and Otto. Famous palindromes and bad bumper stickers include "I prefer pi," "A man, a plan, a canal, Panama" and "Able was I ere I saw Elba." In fact, this entire entry has been written as a palindrome. Just kidding.

## Yo Mnomma's Mnemonics:

*The **Palindrome**: The World's Nerdiest Night Club, featuring...*
Music: "Pop," including Swedish supergroup ABBA
Food: "No lemon(s), no melon"
Drink: BYOYB (Bring Your Own Yoo-hoo Bottles)

# Yo momma's so old, she makes Skeletor look young when they're juxtaposed!

> **jux·ta·pose** (JUKS tuh pohs)
> v. To place side by side (often to show contrast)

Things that are **juxtaposed** are placed side by side. Common usage adds to this basic meaning a goal of illuminating a comparison or contrast: The new iPod Shuffle's **diminutive** (see p. 40) size was evident when juxtaposed with the old one. Weight loss pill **charlatans** (see p. 126) juxtapose **apocryphal** (see p. 95) "Before" and "After" photos to show the effectiveness of their product.

**Yo momma's** hands are so **turgid**, she uses
a hula hoop as a pinkie ring!

**tur·gid** (TUR jid)
adj. Swollen

From *$25,000 Pyramid:*

"A bladder…  varicose veins…"
"Uh…  body parts you should cover up?"
"A swollen broken hand… um…  Overblown pompous prose…"
"Things Mike Tyson might use…"
"A starving child's belly… professors' lectures… Tom Cruise's ego"
"Things that are turgid!"

**Turgid** means swollen, **distended** (see p. 67), especially from
fluid or gas.   Like most words that describe something physical,
turgid, by extension, can mean inflated, overblown, or pompous;
bombastic ("turgid language").


**Yo momma's** so **troglodytic**, she drives a
chariot to work!  Snap!

**trog·lo·dy·tic** (trahg luh DIT ik)
adj. Living in a cave; adhering to an old, outmoded way of
thinking or living

**Troglodytes** are cave-dwellers, usually (and obviously) ancient
ones.  You don't, however, have to restrict your usage to that very
specific definition.  A troglodyte can, more generally, be someone
who keeps to him or herself, or who clings to an outlook that
doesn't quite fit our day and age.  The Ku Klux Klan is
**troglodytic**.  A basketball player who shoots free throws
underhanded?  A little troglodytic.  A teacher who uses those
plastic transparencies on top of a projector is also a little bit of a
troglodyte, but might be more accurately characterized as
something of a **Luddite** (see p. 9).

Sometimes, a momma isn't soooooo anything. She's rather common and unexceptional. Everything about her is **banal**.

**ba·nal** [buh NAL (rhymes with canal)]
or (BAY nuhl)
adj. Commonplace, ordinary to the point of being uninteresting

When you find a momma with banal tastes, you need an **armamentarium** (arsenal, quiver, Glock-ful) of specialized snaps that illuminate the soul-crushing beige of her ordinary life:

**Yo momma** eats Cheerios with milk!

**Yo momma** likes watching Will Smith movies!

**Yo momma** thinks gas is expensive!

**Yo momma** finds clothes at reasonable prices at Old Navy!

**Yo momma** thinks the Cajun Chicken Sandwich at TGI Fridays is pretty good!

**Yo momma** sleeps 7.5 hours a night!

**Yo momma** cooks turkey on Thanksgiving!

**Yo momma** is such a **philistine**, she thought
*Crime and Punishment* was a WWE tagteam!

**phil·is·tine** (FILL uh steen)
n. Someone with no knowledge of or interest in culture
adj. Having no knowledge of or interest in culture, lowbrow

Yo momma thinks the Missouri Compromise is an NBA team.
To her, a night of culture is watching *Real World/Road Rules
Challenge*. She cannot differentiate between jazz songs: there is
one song, and it is called "Jazz." Two wines: "Red" and "White."
She looks at modern art and immediately hollers,
"I could do that." The only culture she gets is when she's tested
for strep. And worse, she doesn't care about her ignorance.
Yo momma is a **philistine**.

**Yo momma's** so dumb, you told her you enjoyed
**persiflage**, and she bought you a hunting outfit.

**per·si·flage** (PER si flahj)
n. Playful, teasing talk, done in a light tone

**Persiflage** is a great word that, contrary to yo momma's ideas,
has nothing to do with camouflage. You and your friends probably
engage in persiflage more often than not. Think about how you
might interact with your best friend, who just got some brand new
red shoes. This is persiflage:

Nice shoes.
What's wrong with them?
With your white socks, you look like a barber pole.
Like you know what a barber pole looks like, Bob Ross.

Trading yo momma jokes is a form of persiflage. Similar words
are **banter** and **badinage**.

Fill the blanks in these TV descriptions with the appropriate word from the list below:

Words: voracious, Luddites, reprobate, double entendres, juxtaposed, **ascetic** (see p. 132)

**Yo Momma's** *TV Guide:*

1. *Three's Company*: Jack, Janet, and Chrissy discuss how they can be better communicators, putting an end to all _____.

2. *Amish Eye for the Modern Guy*: Each week Amish _____ give a modern man's life an extreme _____ make-over in categories ranging from home decorating (tearing out plumbing, removing electricity, collaboratively building a barn) to fashion (dressing him in black, removing buttons in favor of hooks).

3. *The Biggest Luger*: A **corpulent** man and a tiny sled are _____.

4. *Sesame Street*: Cookie Monster admits to his therapist that his _____ appetite stems from paternal abandonment. (This episode caused the letter "r" to pull its sponsorship.)

5. *The Ugly Duckling*: *The Swan* meets *Kids Say the Darndest Things* when _____ parents, who think their average-looking kids aren't attractive enough, hire Los Angeles's most accomplished plastic surgeons to make over their "ugly ducklings."

*Answers: 1) double entendres 2) Luddites, ascetic 3) juxtaposed 4) voracious 5) reprobate*

# Yo momma's so **esophoric**, her tears run down her back!

**esophoric** (ess o FOUR ik)
adj. Cross-eyed

In general, we don't believe in using long, fancy words when a simpler one will do. However, sometimes it's fun to know the more "official" and "scientific" words for common concepts, whether you're parodying **grandiloquent** (see p. 75) prose or trying to disguise your insult. Take the word **esophoric**, which simply means "cross-eyed."

---

### *Word to Your Mother!*

When talking to people with extreme **esophoria**, it is not possible to engage their gaze directly. Rather, pretend you have a phone number on a scrap of paper in your pockets. Carry on the conversation normally, but search for that paper! Jam your hands in, pull things out and examine. If you find paper or a phone number, don't worry—that's not the one! Keep chatting until you have to give up the search. Then say "Oh crap! I'm going to lose my job." Walk away.

---

# Yo momma is such a **procrastinator**, you don't have a name yet!

**pro·cras·tin·a·tor** (pruh CRASS tin ay tuhr)
or (pro CRASS tin ay tuhr)
n. One who delays in doing something or postpones work (often out of laziness)

To **procrastinate** is to put something off, to delay in doing something. We tend to procrastinate when there is something to do that is unpleasant, boring, or daunting. (Note: Finish this entry later.)

**Yo momma's** so dishonest, she **dissembles** at confession.

> **dis·sem·ble**  (dis SEM bul)
> v. To hide one's reason(s) for saying or doing something, or to conceal one's feelings or beliefs

In a media-saturated society, this word is a must.  When they're being interviewed, filmed, or quoted, people are dissembling all over the place.  That's to say, everybody's polished: Everybody knows what to say when the public will hear all of it, and opinions dissolve in a massive wave of **dissembling**.  "I did not have sexual relations with that woman, Miss Lewinsky."

**Yo momma** lives so **vicariously**, I have to insult *you!*

> **vi·car·i·ous**  (vye CARE ee uhs)
> adj. Experienced through imagined participation in the actions or accomplishments of others

After the weight of the world has crushed his spirit, a father can live **vicariously** through his son by attending his football games and remembering days of his own youth, now long gone. The father's only joy comes via his son's achievements, which he experiences as if they were his own.  The common phenomenon of parents living vicariously through their children has resulted in countless familial conflicts and a number of really bad off-Broadway plays.  The billion-dollar Hollywood gossip industry proves that we live vicariously through the lives of celebrities, not to mention that we all enjoy a hefty dose of **schadenfreude** (see p. 53).

# What Has Yo Momma Taught You So Far?

Fill in the blanks with the word that best disses yo momma.

**1. Yo momma's** such a _____, when she goes to KFC, she licks other people's fingers!
   a) sybarite
   b) saprophyte
   c) parasite
   d) sunnydelite

**2. Yo momma's** so _____, she could do a cartwheel and kick angels!
   a) corpulent
   b) grandiloquent
   c) Brobdingnagian
   d) Harriet Tubman

**3. Yo momma's** so _____, she can't even put her two cents in during conversation.
   a) flippant
   b) apathetic
   c) indigent
   d) turgid

**4. Yo momma's** measurements are 36-24-36, but that's for her _____ feet!
   a) turgid
   b) vestigial
   c) banal
   d) sploof

# Yo momma's so nasty, some day, her name will be an **eponym** for ugly! That's right, fool! Eponym!

**ep·o·nym** (EPP uh nihm)

n. A word based on or derived from a person's name

Charles Dickens's *A Christmas Carol* gave us the term "scrooge," born from the **eponymous** character Ebenezer Scrooge and meaning "a miserly, tight-fisted person." The **eponym** "mesmerize" comes from F.A. Mesmer's uncanny ability to hypnotize people. Likewise, "galvanize," "maverick," "sadist," and "thespian" all derive their meaning from the name of a person. An eponym you don't hear much? "Jesusish." What will the eponyms of the future be?

**The eponyms of tomorrow:**

**macgyver** (muh GUY ver)

v. [from the character MacGyver, from the show of the same name] To make the most of limited resources, to an almost magical degree; to create the complex out of the simple and everyday. "He macgyvered a handful of facts into a prize-winning report."

**trebek** (truh BEK)

v or n. [from Alex Trebek, host of *Jeopardy!*] To overarticulate pompously. "He trebeked the phrase 'pièce de résistance,' and was beaten to a bloody pulp."

2. any person given to trebeking; **trebekish**, **trebekese**.

**simpsonize** (SIMP suh neyes)

v. [from O.J. Simpson and Ashlee Simpson] To blame someone else for a mistake, an infraction, or a crime that you obviously committed.

(cont'd on next page)

**The eponyms of tomorrow** [cont'd]:

### baldwinian series (bald WIN ee uhn)

n. [from Hollywood's Baldwin brothers] A series of related specimens that increase incrementally in quality. "The real estate agent showed the prospective buyers a baldwinian series of homes that started with a ramshackle apartment and culminated in a mansion."

### hung [HUHNG]

adj. or n. [from *American Idol* contestant William Hung] **Egregiously** (see p. 7) yet uncaringly incompetent, or a person who exhibits this quality.

### pac-man [PAK man]

adj. & n. [from the arcade game Pac-Man by Bally] Of, pertaining to, or characteristic of a relationship whereby the chaser and the chasee alternatively exchange places: "a pac-man attraction, a pac-man battle."

### vanna [VAN uh]

n. [from Vanna White, co-host of the game show *Wheel of Fortune*] Someone or something that provides little or no function and merely serves decorative purpose.

### weeble [WEE buhl]

n. [from toddler toy the Weeble by Fisher Price] Someone or something that is able to withstand outside forces by wobbling, but never falling down. "In the face of personal scandal and impeachment, Bill Clinton proved to be a political weeble."

### reeses [REE sis]

n. [from Reese's Peanut Butter Cups] An unexpectedly appealing or effective combination. "Mitch and Mildred's thirty years of marriage proves that Mitch's straight-laced personality and Mildred's eccentric tendencies amount to a reeses."

# Yo momma's so **sanguine**, her glass is so half-full, it spilled over!

**san·guine** (SANG wihn)
adj. Enthusiastically optimistic

**Sanguine** means having a ruddy, red, healthy complexion and, by extension, it means "cheerfully optimistic." You tend to see and hear it used in this latter way (e.g. "a sanguine disposition").

*Note to self: Children's book idea: The **Sanguine** Penguin... about a lovably optimistic penguin who sees the best in every situation—even when he is eaten by a polar bear. As he's being devoured, he joyfully realizes that it's all a part of the circle of life.*

# Yo momma's so fat, she told the doctor she needed an **anodyne** for her feet, and he told her to sit down!

**an·o·dyne** (ANN uh dine)
n. A pain-killer (drug or medicine)
adj. Inoffensive or uncontroversial; unlikely to provoke

The more broad usage of **anodyne** is to describe things that don't offend. The band Uncle Tupelo, which gave alternative rock an infusion of country in the early 1990's, named their final album *Anodyne*. Perhaps the title was **ironic** (see p. 117), as the band's soulful rock with a twang flew in the face of much of Nashville's popular sound—slick, poppy country. Or maybe it was a more earnest and accurate usage, as the two helmsmen of the group, Jeff Tweedy and Jay Farrar, were increasingly at odds with each other, and the album, quite an achievement, was something that dulled the **acrimony** (bitterness) between them and served as an anodyne of sorts.

# An **Exercise** in **Ambivalence**

**am·biv·a·lent** (am BIHV uh luhnt)
adj. Lacking the ability to decide; having generally mixed feelings about something

In the classic literary tome, *Would You Rather...?*, the authors present a series of dilemmas that place readers in between the rockiest of rocks and the hardest of hard places. The result: As readers attempt to decide which fate they'd prefer, they experience a great deal of **ambivalence**. See if you are able to wade through your ambivalence and make a decision when confronted with the following dilemmas:

Would you rather...
fight Mike Tyson
or
talk like him?

Would you rather...
be stoned to death by pickles
or
be submerged in mayonnaise until you die?

Would you rather...
be able to simulate the hair of anyone you meet
or
simulate the hairstyle?

Would you rather...
sneeze with the force of a double-barrel shotgun
or
snore the sound of a dial-up modem?

# Yo momma's so **fastidious**, she fact-checks menus!

**fas·tid·i·ous** (fas TIHD ee uhs)
adj. Characterized by a heightened attention to detail;
hard to please

If you're a **fastidious** writer or speaker, you choose your words carefully and deliberately. It's important to you always to say the right thing. You might. Even. Take a while. In doing so. Diane Lane's **fastidiously** outlined memorandum for her on-location acting work has been documented online by The Smoking Gun: freshly-squeezed juice twice a day and a personal yoga instructor, among other requirements. Her demands reflect both definitions of fastidious, actually: she is being very particular down to the last detail *and* hard to please. Fastidious refers to a certain type of "hard to please"—demanding, picky, etc., whereas the word **captious** (see below) suggests a slightly different shade of the "hard to please" idea. This is the beauty of learning new words from *Yo Momma*—you can now more precisely express your ideas.

# Yo momma's so **captious**, the U.S. Geological Survey hired her to find faults!

**cap·tious** (CAP shus)
adj. Hard to please; often finding fault and raising
trivial objections

Aside from the **schadenfreude** (see p. 53) derived from watching hopefuls embarrass themselves, *American Idol's* biggest draw is its **captious** host, Simon Cowell. He rarely has anything good to say. He's the judge everyone fears. He **captiously** criticizes the style, appearance and delivery of nearly every *Idol*-wannabe's performance. Paula Abdul on the other hand is more **mawkish** (see p. 84) than captious; Randy Jackson, always trying to strike a balance between Cowell and Abdul, can at times be **effusive** (see p. 39).

**Yo momma's** gut is so **distended**, when she lies down, people yell, "Hey Big Top!"

**dis·tend** (dis TEND)
v. To swell as a result of interior pressure

The most important thing to remember about the word **distended** is that it doesn't mean "fat." In this example, yo momma's *gut* is distended—not yo momma. You might say that since she's so fat, yo momma is host to a symphony of distended organs and body parts, but it's usually inaccurate to say that yo momma is distended. A good exception might be Violet in *Willy Wonka and the Chocolate Factory* when she swells into a blueberry. Or the guy in Monty Python's *The Meaning of Life* who explodes after tipping the scales with that last wafer-thin mint: He pushed the limits of his own **distensibilty** too far.

**Yo momma's** so dumb, she **advocated** a fat tax.

**ad·vo·cate** (ADD vuh kate) [if noun: (ADD vuh kit)]
v. To support publicly
n. A public supporter

There's a certain degree of visibility to **advocacy**. "**Advocates** of change" are often public protesters. If you're **advocating**, you're telling people about it by writing editorials or making speeches or disseminating information. Union members, advocating better wages, picket with signs scrawled with slogans (except those from the Writers Guild, whose signs are blank).

**Sampling:**

*Millard staunchly **advocated** legislation to end pinflation (the unnecessary increase in the scale of pinball scores).*

# Yo momma's so **utilitarian**, she doesn't see a glass half empty or half full, she sees it as twice as big as it needs to be!

**u·til·i·tar·i·an** (yoo tihl ih TARE ee uhn)
adj. Useful rather than pretty or showy

Yo **utilitarian** momma is practical. She's a pragmatist. She simply sees that the glass is bigger than it needs to be. Children's books often feature freaks with deformities—Rudolph the Red-Nosed Reindeer, for example, or our favorite, Flat Stanley. Flat Stanley was a kid who was paper thin, virtually two-dimensional. Like Rudolph, he was the victim of much **castigation** (see p. 90), until the other kids realized he had utilitarian value, such as the ability to retrieve a lost ball by slipping down into a sewer. Similarly, Rudolph's red nose served the utilitarian purpose of helping Santa navigate through the fog. Dumbo was mocked for his big ears until they allowed him to fly. And this is the lesson repeatedly told in children's books: Make fun of freaks until their deformity reveals a utilitarian purpose.

# Yo momma's so **depraved**, she ordered a pizza to a funeral.

**de·prave** (duh PRAYV)
v. To make immoral, to corrupt
[n.: **depravity** (duh PRAV uh tee), where "PRAV" sounds like the "av" in "avenue," "gravity," "avalanche," "avatar" and "cavalcade"]

So this is the depth of yo momma's **depravity**. She is both immoral and off in the head. People who are **depraved** often are associated with worse things than what yo momma does above, actually. (Maybe if she charged the delivery to the deceased—then we'd be getting close.) Corrupt and murderous leaders such as Saddam Hussein often are described as depraved.

# Yo Daddy!

**Yo daddy's** so **polygamous**, he buys his wedding rings in bulk!

**po·lyg·a·my** (puh LIG uh mee)
[adj. is **polygamous** (puh LIG uh muhs)]
n. The state or practice of having multiple spouses

That's right, yo daddy wears so many wedding rings, he can't even crack his knuckles. On TV's *The Bachelor*, the bachelor starts out **polygamous** (dating multiple women) and ends up **monogamous** (dating one). If you want to get technical, he is never truly polygamous, because that would mean he'd actually be *married* to more than one woman. And that would be sleazy, unlike dating dozens of women simultaneously and then randomly deciding which one he "loves" after dinner.

**Yo daddy's** so **predatory**, he goes to the self-help section at a bookstore to hit on women!

**pred·a·tor·y** (PRED uh tor ee)
adj. Characterized by exploiting or victimizing others

**Predatory** obviously is the adjective form of **predator**. In the world of zoology, predators prey upon other animals for food. Someone who is predatory preys upon other people in some way. In the case of yo daddy, as described above, he preys upon insecure females looking for answers from self-help books. Yo daddy waits like a predator, lurking behind the bookshelf, and strikes just at the right time with an **insidious** (see p. 129) sensitivity. Predatory con artists send spam soliciting money transfers into Nigerian bank accounts. Such predatory schemes aim to capitalize on the **largesse** (see p. 6) of some ignorant person.

## Don't Be So **Flippant**

**flip·pant** (FLIP uhnt)
adj. Marked by or displaying disrespectful or
inappropriate levity

When you don't give the appropriate respect to a serious matter,
you're being **flippant**. If you call your boss "Daddio," you're
being flippant. If you start a "Bo-ring" chant at a funeral,
that's being flippant. Joking around and being snide are fine in
certain situations, but, in the wrong context, you can come off
as flippant. It's kind of like using the Spanish "tu" form when
you should be using the formal "usted."

The following poems are the ultimate in flippant remarks for
some very serious circumstances, as they use the light, bouncy,
whimsical style of Dr. Seuss to address some important
situations.

**"I'm sorry, sir. You have six months to live."**
Your heart is pumping
Your heart is popping
But in one year and a half
Your heart will be stopping
It'll clonk, it'll clank
It'll cloink, it'll clunk
And then your body will fall
Just like that – kerplunk!
And you'll be tossed in the ground
With all sorts of junk.

**"I just don't love you anymore."**
I do not love you anymore
I do not love you when you snore
I do not love you in the sack
I do not love you with a yak
I do not love you on a plane
I do not love you in the rain
I do not love you in sleet or snow
I do not love you when barometric pressure is low
I do not love you in the fall
I do not love you under any meteorological conditions at all
I do not love you on Yom Kippur
I just don't love you anymore
Not in the leastest the very most leastest
The lesser than least of the very most leastest
There's nothing for me to love you for
I just don't love you anymore.

**"You're fired."**
Clean out your in-box
And jump in your out-box
Wipe clear your desk
And forget all your stocks
They've been locked away
With ten thousand lox
And just for good measure
An arctic snow fox
So goodbye and sorry
If you feel disgraced
That you and three others have all been replaced
By a 16 year old with spots on his face.

# Yo momma's so old, she has a **vestigial** tail!

**ves·tig·ial** (ves TI jee uhl) or (ves TIJ uhl)
adj. Showing a trace of something that no longer exists or is no longer practiced

Doctors wonder what the **vestigial** appendix might have once been used for. The wigs still worn in British courts are **vestiges** of an earlier time. When the rare video shows on MTV, it is a vestige of the network's original music television concept, before it began showing 15 shows about moderately attractive 20-somethings eking out a living by being drunk on camera and competing in obstacle course races. In such dark times, we hang on to the last vestige of hope that entertainment may someday again be tolerable.

## What Should Be The Word Origin But Isn't:

In Ancient Rome, there lived a ruler named King **Vestiges**. King Vestiges was determined to leave a legacy worthy of his reign. To this end, the king built a massive palace and, in its center, he erected an inner sanctum with 20-foot-thick sandstone walls. However, his preoccupation with posterity caused him to neglect the growing discontent of his people. Feeling their concerns were being ignored, the incensed countrymen attacked the palace of Vestiges. The temple was destroyed in battle and King Vestiges was killed, but the ruins of the inner sanctum still stood. "There lives Vestiges!" the former king's supporters would proclaim. "And that is all that remains," his detractors would answer. Vestiges soon took on the meaning of "the last remaining traces of something no longer present." Of course, this whole story is entirely bogus. It's not the word origin at all, but it should be!

# What Has Yo Momma Taught You So Far?

Choose from the following words to complete the statement that best describes the reason for the person's death.

Words: *Procrastinating, Gauche, Incredulous*

**1.** Scientist Barry Melch was the first person to successfully transplant the brain of Martha Stewart into an 800 pound gorilla. At a recent tea party thrown by the gorilla, Melch belched loudly, forgot to use a coaster, and used the wrong knife to spread marmalade on his cranberry scone. The gorilla flew into a rage and tore Barry Melch's head from his body... then used his skull to make a festive holiday candy dish.

Barry Melch died because of his _____ behavior.

**2.** At age 37, Josh Greenberg was diagnosed by his doctor as having a common and easily curable flu virus. The doctor recommended a mild antibiotic, plenty of fluids and a few days of rest. Mr. Greenberg's response was as follows: "I don't believe that I'm sick! Even if I were, which I'm not, I don't believe that I need any medicine or fluids. Furthermore, I don't think that you are even a real doctor!" His dying words were: "I'm NOT dying!"

Josh Greenberg died because he was _____.

**3.** At the age of 6, Stevie Brooks was told by his mother to change his shirt. Stevie said that he would get to it, but he never did. Twelve years and 130 pounds later, Stevie was slowly strangled to death by the extra-small child-size Power Rangers shirt that he was still wearing.

Stevie Brooks died from his _____.

*Answers: 1. Gauche, 2. Incredulous, 3. Procrastinating*

Movie studios don't always go with their first choice for a film's title. Complete the rejected film title for the following real films by using the following words:

Words: *Jaundiced, Reprobates, Homely, Procrastinating, Comely*

**1.** _____ *Woman* - A businessman needs an escort for some social events, and hires a beautiful prostitute he meets... only to fall in love.

**2.** *Coyote* _____ - A down on her luck songwriter comes out of her shell when she gets a job at a bar where women dance suggestively on the bar and perform other wild antics.

**3.** _____ *Submarine* - The Beatles agree to accompany Captain Fred in his Yellow Submarine and go to Pepperland to free it from the music-hating Blue Meanies.

**4.** *Dirty Rotten* _____ - Lawrence and Freddie are con men. After working together and swindling women out of their fortunes, they realize that this French Mediterranean town ain't big enough for the two of 'em.

**5.** _____ *to Exhale* - Friendship becomes the strongest bond between four African-American women as men, careers, and families take them in different directions.

*Answers:* 1) *Comely Woman* 2) *Coyote Homely* 3) *Jaundiced Submarine* 4) *Dirty Rotten Reprobates* 5) *Procrastinating to Exhale*

74    The Yo Momma Vocabulary Builder

**Yo momma's** delivery is so **grandiloquent**, by the time she finishes ordering food, it's time for dessert!

**gran·dil·o·quent** (gran DIL uh kwent)
adj. Expressed in an elaborate or pompous style

**Grandiloquent** speech is self-important, taking the long and extravagant way around to making a point, usually with the aim of impressing. Matt Lauer, a guy who wants everybody to relate to him, uses speech that is not grandiloquent; Matthew McConaughey, who sometimes presents himself as something of a "life teacher," occasionally does ("Life is a series of commas, not periods"). Grandiloquence is usually a sign of amateurish speaking and thought. A simple rule: If you find yourself using the word grandiloquent, chances are your delivery is way too grandiloquent.

**Sampling:**

*The pompous second grader* **grandiloquently** *asked for his kickball pitch to be "undulating, with an exceeding amount of velocity."*

**Yo momma's** teeth are so **askew**, it looks like her mouth's throwing up gang signs.

**a·skew** (uh SKYOO)
adj. & adv. Not level or even

**Askew** is a special kind of crooked, meaning turned or twisted to one side. A picture can be knocked askew on a wall. A tie can be askew if not tied right. Ashton Kutcher thinks it's cool to wear a baseball cap askew, presumably to shield his preferred eye from the sun. (Not sure if he wears his yarmulke askew to a Bar Mitzvah.) Note that askew can be an adjective ("that askew picture") or an adverb ("the picture was hanging askew").

# Aphorisms Left Out Of *Chicken Soup for the Soul*

An **aphorism** (AFF uhr ism) is a concise saying that expresses an idea, opinion, or piece of wisdom. Examples of **aphorisms** are "A bird in the hand is worth two in the bush," "A stitch in time saves nine," and "All that glitters is not gold." Aphorisms are used to instruct and sometimes inspire. However, the aphorisms below are meant to do the opposite. These are **cynical** aphorisms (or those based on believing in the worst of human nature).

**Cynical aphorisms:**

- It takes ten years to make an overnight failure.

- Success is failure turned inside out (by someone substantially smarter than you).

- Life is killing time between meals.

- He who seeks only money is the poorest of all in a vague, insignificant way.

- I've found a little remedy to ease the life we live and make each day a happier one; it is the word "vengeance."

- Actions speak louder than words, and accordingly take much more time and effort, which are not pleasing to expend.

- You only need more because you think you don't have enough. That and you get bogged down in semantics all the time.

- Laughter is the best medicine for Christian Scientists.

# Yo momma's so **obtuse**, she puts stamps on faxes!

**ob·tuse** (ahb TOOS) or (ahb TYOOS)
adj. Slow to understand or perceive; difficult to understand

If yo momma is **obtuse**, she is slow to catch on. She sits on the TV and watches the couch. It takes her an hour to cook minute rice, etc. Yo momma is not sharp. Obtuse is a word with definite **pejorative** (see p. 140) connotations. Usually, if someone merits being called obtuse, he or she has somehow frustrated you. In *The Shawshank Redemption*, Tim Robbins's character Andy Dufresne, imprisoned for killing his wife—a crime he didn't commit—calls the warden "obtuse" when the warden refuses to believe a story that would've **exonerated** him, or freed him from all suspicion of having committed the crime. Obtuse's other meaning indicates that something is hard to decipher, like Bob Dylan's obtuse song lyrics, or the **obtuseness** of advanced calculus, or the M.C. Escher-like **paradox** (see p. 87) that is Donald Trump's hair.

# Yo momma's so **asinine**, when you said it was chilly outside, she ran out with a spoon.

**as·i·nine** (ASS uh nine)
adj. Stupid, foolish

The biggest difference between **obtuse** and **asinine** is that asinine usually applies to behavior. That is, someone doesn't have to be stupid to be asinine. At the 2006 Winter Olympics, many described the behavior of free-spirited U.S. downhiller Bode Miller, who claimed to have been out partying on the nights prior to races he competed in, as **egregiously** (see p. 7) and selfishly asinine.

## Yo Mnomma's Mnemonics:

*The show Jackass and its merry cast of pain-seekers have created an entire industry built on asinine antics. Think Jack-asinine.*

**Yo momma** is so **monomaniacal** about tech stock investing, I was like, "What's up?" and she was like, "NASDAQ-listed CDC Corp., 6.3%!"

**mon·o·ma·ni·ac·al** (mahn uh muh NYE uh kuhl) n. Excessively obsessed with one particular thing to the exclusion of everything else

Maybe yo momma's really into NASCAR. If that's the case, she'd know everything about the drivers—where they live, what their wives look like, what their chances are in the next race (based, of course, on her penetrating knowledge of their engine capabilities and the skills of their crews). But that's the key: It's not just that she knows everything about NASCAR, but that she's so into it she does things like miss your wedding and burn your dinner and forget your name. She's **monomaniacal** about NASCAR. That tunnel vision, that one-track mind, makes it **monomania**. Cesar Millan, the "Dog Whisperer," is monomanical about dogs. George Washington Carver, regarded as an important historical figure until you get past fifth grade, was a tad monomaniacal about the peanut. Put the nut down, George, and get some fresh air.

So monomania signifies a one-track obsession with anything. **Megalomania** (meg uh loh MAY nee uh) indicates an obsessive delusion regarding one's own importance or power. Hitler has been characterized as a **megalomaniac**. So has Michael Eisner, the former helmsman of Disney. Ever heard of John Lennon's famous remark that the Beatles were "more popular than Jesus"? That might shut the door on all other **megalomaniacal** proclamations.

**Monomaniac, Megalomaniac or Both?**
- Martha Stewart
- Tiger Woods
- Terrell Owens
- That guy at the Mac store that spoke to you about the advantages of the new operating system for 2 hours

## Guess the meaning of the words based on the snap!

**Yo momma's** so **omniscient**, she put on a pair of Guess jeans and knew the answer!

**Yo momma's** so **vacuous**, she imploded!

**Yo momma's** so **peripatetic**, she went out for a walk and never came back!

**Yo momma's** so **xenophobic**, she called it quits when her fourth child was born, because she read that every fifth child born is Chinese!

**Yo momma's** so **penurious**, she eats cereal with a fork to save milk.

*Answers: 1. Omniscient - knowing everything; 2. Vacuous - having no contents (lacking any meaning or substance); 3. Peripatetic - traveling from place to place, wandering; 4. Xenophobic - having an unreasonable fear or hatred of foreigners or foreign things; 5. Penurious - extremely frugal, cheap*

Fill in the blanks.

**1.** The _____ Hollywood superagent gave a smooth, polished pitch, fooling the naïve studio executive with a _____ argument about how people can't get enough movies about a robot fighting crime with an aristocratic butler.

   a) salacious, agnostic

   b) specious, unctuous

   c) unctuous, specious

   d) agnostic, impassive

**2.** If the only "dis" I want to give **yo momma** is "antidisetablishmentarianism," I am _____.

   a) moribund

   b) sesquipedalian

   c) effusive

   d) Harriet Tubman

**3.** If **yo momma's** waist size is larger than her IQ, she is likely both _____ and _____.

   a) corpulent, obtuse

   b) indigent, gauche

   c) fallopian, unseld

   d) orange, adhesive

*Answers: 1c; 2b; 3a*

# If Musicians had Better Vocabularies

"I like **callipygian** women, and I cannot
**equivocate**; other brothers might **eschew**
the issue!"

(Paraphrased from Sir Mixalot's "Baby Got Back.")

**cal·li·pyg·i·an** (kal uh PIJ ee uhn)
adj. Having shapely buttocks

**e·quiv·o·cate** (ee KWIV uh kate)
v. To speak purposely in an unclear way

**es·chew** (es CHOO)
v. To avoid, stay away from as a matter of principle
or routine

What's nice about the word **callypigian** is that it sounds like
such a sophisticated, regal word, and yet its actual meaning is far
more base. Like the way "Born in the USA" sounds at first like
a patriotic song, but actually is anything but **jingoistic** (see p.
128). Or how Billy Idol's "White Wedding" is actually an anti-
wedding song. Or the way "We Are The World" is actually a
pro-suicide tune (listen closely).

When politicians speak in an unclear way in order to avoid giving
any real answer, they are being **equivocal**. When running for
office, candidates **equivocate** to avoid offending anyone.

Speaking of "avoid," **eschew** is a fancy word that means to stay
clear of. It's more specific than the word "avoid," in that it generally
refers to a concept or abstract idea rather than a physical object.

**Sampling:**

*Reginald avoided the dish that was thrown at him, realizing
that he should have* **eschewed** *the topic of whether his wife's
new jeans made her posterior look more* **distended** *(see p. 67)
than* **callipygian**.

**Yo momma's** so prone to **anachronism**, she thought an iPod was a preppie shirt!

### anachronism

n. Something or someone in the wrong time period; the act of attributing something or someone to such an erroneous time period

Yo momma belongs in the 1980's. She wears pink collared shirts, parts her hair in the middle, wears high-waisted belts…. What? That's cool again? Oh. Sometimes, someone can be such an **anachronism** that he or she is contemporary-retro (pardon the **oxymoron**, see p. 107). Hollywood employs anachronism as the premise of many movies: The rapper sent back in time to the 1950s; the medieval princess who changes places with a present-day baby-sitter, or the conquistador who has been magically transported to work in a modern day Radio Shack. In Colonial Williamsburg, Va., you can spot **anachronisms** if you look closely, like a blacksmith wearing Reeboks.

## Quizzle

**Can you spot the anachronism in each group?**

1. a) Drive-in movie theaters
   b) Poodle skirts
   c) The Spanish Armada
   d) Elvis

2. a) Blue beverages in weirdly shaped glasses
   b) Cheeky robots
   c) A Commodore 64
   d) Pocketless form-fitting uniforms

3. a) Hybrid cars
   b) Flat screen TV's
   c) YouTube.com
   d) The cotton gin

4. a) Thomas Jefferson
   b) Alexander Hamilton
   c) Benjamin Franklin
   d) Bob Costas

*Answers: 1c; 2c; 3d; 4d*

# Yo momma's such a **hedonist**, she bathes in chocolate!

**he·don·ist** (HEEd nist) or (HEE duh nist)
n. One who embraces the idea that sensual pleasure is the ultimate aim in life

You could interpret the above snap to be another slam regarding yo momma's **corpulence** (see p. 4) and **voracious** (see p. 3) appetite. But then we could have said that she bathes in nougat or butter. We chose chocolate specifically because it is a symbol of pleasure. **Hedonists** are pleasure-seekers. Their pleasure can come in **myriad** (countless) forms: food, flesh, drink, etc. Eddie Murphy sang about his girl who had a tendency to party all the time, party all the time, party all the tie-yime, and, therefore, was a hedonist, hedonist, heeee-yeeedonist. Rappers cultivate **hedonistic** images, swilling bottles of champagne as they sit around pools surrounded by bikini-clad women.

# Yo momma's so **soporific**, doctors use her for anesthesia!

**sop·o·rif·ic** (sahp uh RIFF ik)
adj. Boring or monotonous; inducing sleep

Things described as **soporific** can make somebody fall asleep. Some drugs are medically described as **soporifics**, meaning that they cause you to fall asleep. But the real mileage the word gets you is by describing things that can induce sleep, mind-numbing things that are **soporifically** boring. C-Span is soporific. Many people consider John Kerry's speeches to be soporific. Or soporifics can literally cause sleep, like the motion of the sea when you're on a raft, or warm milk, or, for some people, flying on a plane. Bob Ross, the painter with the red afro on PBS, was pleasantly soporific, his calm voice the perfect lullaby to bring on a nap. Perhaps a coiled lock of his **hirsute** (see p. 2) halo could be magically distilled into a soporific drug.

# Yo momma's snore is so **cacophonous**,
she sounds like a dial-up modem!

**ca·coph·o·ny** (kuh KOFF uh nee)
adj. Harsh-sounding, composed of a disagreeable sound or sounds

Think of **cacophony** (the noun form) as the opposite of harmony: a collection of discordant, often unpleasant sounds like you might find in the rainforest or on a Morning Zoo radio show. Certain punk rock bands purposely create a **cacophonous** sound. **Cacophonies** don't only have to describe literal sounds: OutKast's Andre 3000 is widely considered one of the finest dressers in entertainment; his detractors claim, however, that plaids stacked on top of stripes, as well as so many battling bright colors, all matched up with hockey boots, create a cacophony of styles and hues.

# Yo momma's so **mawkish**, she cries when
she talks about breakfast!

**mawk·ish** (MAWK ish)
adj. Excessively and overly sentimental, so much so that nausea or loathing can result

**Mawkishness** is not a quality you want. You're sentimental to the point that everybody knows it. You cry at Hallmark cards and long distance commercials. You dig up unreasonably strong emotions when you **mawkishly** recall, at length, the drama of a middle-school soccer game. Romance novels and soap operas are usually **mawkish**, as well as some of the exceedingly in-your-face declarations of love you see with couples on *The O.C.* A synonym is **maudlin**.

## Sampling:
*The hair band alternated between angry, **cacophonous** slams and **mawkish** power ballads, finding the perfect combination to exploit the teenage audience.*

# Yo momma is the **apotheosis** of ugliness!

**ap•o•the•o•sis** (uh poth ee OH sis or ap uh THEE uh sis)

n. The elevation of a person to godlike status; an ideal example

**Apotheosis** comes from a Greek word that means "to deify," or "to make a god," and it can take that meaning in English: "People credit the teen universe's apotheosis of Britney Spears to generation-wide tone-deafness." It's more commonly used to mean an ideal example: "The average contestant on *The Apprentice* is the apotheosis of **obsequiousness** (see p. 125), hoping to kiss his way up Trump's corporate ladder."

A similar word to apotheosis is **epitome**. Note the pronunciation (i PIT uh mee). We could say that yo momma is the epitome of ugliness. An epitome is a perfect representation of a whole class, type, or idea. If we looked up "ugly" in the dictionary, there wouldn't be a picture of yo momma, but only because it's too ugly to print. We could also say yo momma is the **quintessence** of ugliness, which means she is the "pure essence" of ugliness.

## Quizzle

Each person or thing listed below on the left is the **epitome/quintessence/apotheosis** of one item listed on the right.

| | |
|---|---|
| a. Hitler | Cajun Cooking |
| b. Leonardo da Vinci | 1980's Romantic Comedy |
| c. *Sixteen Candles* | Evil |
| d. Emeril | Renaissance Man |

*Answers: a. Evil; b. Renaissance Man; c. Comedy; d. Cajun Cooking (Though for fun, **juxtapose** (see p. 54) the incorrect answers and imagine.)*

# EXTRA EXTRA!

## Superfluous DVD Features

DVD's of movies often feature "extras": supplementary features such as extended footage, behind-the-scenes segments, cast interviews, etc. However, surveys reveal that only 10% of the public actually ends up watching the extras. This is mainly because the extras are just thrown onto the DVD with no real value to the viewer. When something is extra, but really unnecessary, we say it's **superfluous**.

**su•per•flu•ous** (suh PER floo uhs)
adj. Unnecessary, more than is needed

**Would you find these DVD extras superfluous?**

*Star Wars Trilogy*: Deluxe Edition—2 discs of Extras!

- Sequence in which a young Skywalker uses the force to make Eggs Benedict
- Chewbacca's lengthy shower and shampoo scene
- Montage of Boba Fett's failed accounting career
- Special Documentary: *Making of the Star Wars Trilogy!*
- Special Documentary: *Making of the Documentary: Making of the Star Wars Trilogy!*
- Voice-over commentary by Chewbacca

*The Godfather*: Collector's Edition—7 Discs of Extras!

- 147 hours of additional footage, including an extended introductory FBI warning, and 35 minutes of Marlon Brando eating cupcakes in his trailer
- Commentary by Italian-Americans who took the movie the wrong way and are psyched up, looking for trouble!
- Languages: English (Dolby 5.1 EX), Spanish (Dolby 2.0 Surround), Spanglish (Dolby 2.0 Surround)!
- Featurette: Al Pacino sits on a bench and recites geometric formulas!

# Yo Momma's Paradox: Yo momma's so dumb, she sold her car for gasoline money!

**par·a·dox** (PAIR uh docks)
adj.  A statement that is seemingly contradictory or absurd, and, yet may be true

OK. This one is complicated, and yet that's what makes it so simple.  A **paradox** is a statement or proposition that seems self-contradictory or absurd, but in reality, expresses a possible truth. What? Huh?!  OK, take it easy.  No one has to get hurt. Look at the definition again.  Take a deep breath.  It's going to be OK.  Stare at the ceiling. Really take in the idea of the paradox.  Only by not thinking about it can you understand it. Blows your mind, huh?   Some examples of **paradoxical** statements are: "You must sometimes be cruel to be kind" and "Doing nothing can be exhausting."

There is another kind of paradox that is even more complicated. Entire books have been written on the concept of **logical paradox**, so we won't attempt to explain it with a definition, which **paradoxically** seems to make it harder to understand the meaning.  Instead, we'll offer an example: "This statement is false." If the statement is false, then what it is saying is not true, so the statement must be true; but if the statement is true, then the statement must be false; but if the statement is false… and so on. (By now your wallet has been stolen.)

This is what the above yo momma joke is hinting at, implying that, if yo momma sells her car for gasoline money, she then has no car to put it in.  As a result, she needs to buy a car with the gas money she just made, but now she has a car but no gas again… This infinite **conundrum** (something that puzzles) is known as **Yo Momma's Paradox**.  This sort of never-ending Pong of a predicament is also sometimes called a catch-22 (see index, p. 161), named for Joseph Heller's book of the same name.

# Yo momma's head's so **depilated**, she gets brainwashed in the shower!

**dep·i·la·ted** (DEP uh layt id)
adj. Bald, hairless; having all the hair removed from

We live in an age of mass **depilation**. So much more than surfboards, bowling alleys, and Olympic swimmers are getting waxed these days. Even guys, ever more frequently, have the urge for someone to depilate their chests, backs, and butts. Joe Namath is most certainly thrilled that his heyday was during the 1960's and 1970's, as he's a pretty **hirsute** (see p. 2) guy. Andre Agassi has a depilated head and a body that's anything but.

# Yo momma's so **apathetic**, she didn't even react when she heard that last joke.

**ap·a·thet·ic** (ap uh THET ik)
adj. Lacking any concern, care, or excitement about anything

I don't care about words or this book. I don't care about anything. I'm **apathetic**. I'm uninterested, unconcerned, and indifferent. In the 1990's, **apathy** was in vogue. The "I don't care" attitude **permeated** (filled and flowed throughout) popular culture. Grunge hits talked about how much bands didn't care about anything and yet, **paradoxically** (see p. 87), the bands ruthlessly desired attention. Many students are apathetic about school because they think it is irrelevant to their lives. Americans are apathetic about politics: A recent survey found that fewer Americans vote than those who answer stupid useless surveys. Apathy is different from **ambivalence**, which means being torn about something, having two coexisting, conflicting feelings or opinions. See page 65 for an exercise in ambivalence.

# Yo Momma's Similes

**si•mi•le** (SIM uh lee)
n. A figure of speech in which two things are
compared (usually using "like" or "as")

**Effective yo momma similes:**

**Yo momma** is like a 10-story multiplex theater playing
nothing but Pauly Shore movies: disappointing on
so many levels.

**Yo momma** is like the sun: If you stare at her too long,
you'll go blind.

**Yo momma** is like an appendix: We could all do
without her.

**Yo momma similes that fall apart halfway through:**

**Yo momma** is like a pineapple: Prickly on the outside,
and sometimes, uh…she is segmented into donut-
shaped sliccs.

**Yo momma** is like the New York Knicks: Hall-of-
famer Willis Reed once played for her!

**Yo momma** is like Weird Al Yankovic: She bears a
striking resemblance to Weird Al Yankovic.

**Yo momma** is like a toothbrush. I'm not sure why.
It's more of a gut feeling than a logic thing.

# Yo Momma's Tasty Leftovers

**Yo momma's** so **insouciant**, I told her to chill out and she went up in temperature!

**in·sou·ci·ant** (in SOO see uhnt)
adj. Unconcerned, carefree, indifferent

**Insouciant** mommas are carefree. They're not quite **apathetic** (see p. 88); they're just casually light-hearted. We could have also said yo momma is **nonchalant**, but it's cool. Whatever.

**Your momma's** so **oblique**, she won a limbo contest by accident!

**ob·lique** (uhb LEEK)
adj. Reclined, slanted

Yo momma is neither perpendicular nor parallel to a given line or surface. She's slanting or sloping, so naturally you'd think she'd win a limbo contest. Because she's slanted.

**Yo momma's** so bitter, she **castigates** Salvation Army volunteers.

**cas·ti·gate** (KASS ti gate)
v. To criticize someone or something harshly; to reprimand or punish severely

When you **castigate** someone, you really let him or her have it. It's more harsh than similar words such as "reprimand" or "scold."

**Yo momma's** so stupid, she tried to commit suicide by **defenestrating** herself... on the first floor!

**De·fen·e·strate** (dee FEN es trate) (Latin "fenestra" means "window")
v. Literally, to throw out the window

Evidently enough people throw people or things out of windows to warrant **defenestrate's** admittance into the English language. In the old days, **defenestrations** started wars. (Read up on the Defenestration of Prague, for example.) It really is a word. What is not a word, however, is "fenestrate," meaning "to throw *into* a window." That just doesn't happen enough: "Gerald selflessly fenestrated his partner into the warehouse before the police opened fire." Or: "Lionel fenestrated the cooling pie onto the kitchen table on his way in from the back yard." **Defenestrate** is a word with a very specific meaning, and if they can have a word for "throw out of a window," then we suggest the dictionary czars admit the following list of words and their meanings.

**Words with really specific meanings that should exist but don't:**

- *martyrvorce* - When someone uses the "it's not you, it's me" excuse to end a relationship

- *wheretigo* - The act of faking out a dog or small baby by putting something behind your back and pretending it's gone

- *sornitate* - To discuss the war of 1812 to C. Thomas Howell (I sornitated at the party for a while before getting some punch.)

- *sploof* - The journey porridge takes from bowl to mouth (The porridge fell out of the spoon during its sploof.)

- *fluck* - A hurried frontal tuck of a shirt

- *lardochondriac* - A person who constantly asks, "Does this make me look fat?"

# What Has Yo Momma Taught You So Far?

**1.** Match the pair with the word that best describes them.

a) Pac-Man & Takeru Kobayashi (the skinny Japanese eating champion)

b) The Incredible Hulk & Ike Turner

c) RuPaul & most anime characters

d) Woody Allen & The Cowardly Lion

e) The cast of *Jackass* and anyone who marries Liza Minnelli

Words: masochistic; voracious; timorous;
**mercurial** (see p. 123); **epicene** (see p. 100)

**2.** Match the song lyrics with word that describes their message.

a) "I want to rock and roll all night and party every day" – Kiss

b) "Ain't nothing gonna break my stride, ain't nothing gonna slow me down" – Matthew Wilder

c) "Don't Worry, Be Happy" – Bobby McFerrin

Words: insouciant; indefatigable; hedonistic

**3.** Match the superhero with his description.

a) Perfunctorio

b) Fast Idious

c) The Esophoric Wonder

- The world's first obsessive-compulsive superhero. Fights crime in an exact, detail-oriented manner.

- Has heat ray vision, but with very unpredictable aim.

- Just goes through the motions when saving the world.

*Answers:*
*1. a) voracious b) mercurial c) epicene d) timorous e) masochistic*
*2. a) hedonistic b) indefatigable c) insouciant*
*3. a) goes through the motions b) obsessive-compulsive c) unpredictable heat vision*

# A good **epithet** for **yo momma**? Sasquatch.

**epithet** (EP uh thet)

n. A phrase that characterizes someone or something (sometimes to substitute for a person's name)

An **epithet** is a word or phrase used to describe something or someone; although it doesn't have to be, an epithet can be, and usually is, a put-down. (Consider the usage you've most likely heard: "racial epithet.") Some **epithetical** examples that aren't insulting: "king of the jungle" (for lion); Alexander the Great; or, as Homer describes Ares, "sacker of cities."

## Quizzle

Which of the following epithets describe characters from *Lord of the Rings* and which are used to describe World Wrestling Entertainment wrestlers?

a. The Brahma Bull

b. Master Stormcrow

c. The Rated "R" Super Star

d. Mighty among both elves and men

e. The Ayatollah of Rock & Rolla

f. The Ugandan Giant

g. Eagle of the Star

h. Evenstar of the people

*Answers: a. WWE (The Rock); b. LOTR (Gandalf); c. WWE (Edge); d. LOTR (Elrond); e. WWE (Chris Jericho); f. WWE (Kamala); g. LOTR (a translation of Thorongil, one of Aragorn's epithets); h. LOTR (Arwen)*

# Yo momma's acronym:

Morbidly Obese Mutant Monkey-Ape.

**ac·ro·nym** (AK roh nihm)
n. A word formed by the initial letters of group of words

Scuba is an **acronym** for "self contained underwater breathing apparatus." If you had to say the whole thing, no one would ever want to go diving. NASA is an acronym for "National Aeronatics and Space Administration." SARS is an acronym for "Severe Acute Respiratory Syndrome." "Boys Entering Anarchistic States Towards Internal Excellence" is the surprising acronymn for the "Beastie" in "Beastie Boys."

**If celebrity names were acronyms:**

- MOBY – Musician Overcoming Baldness Youthfully

- DR. PHIL – **Depilated** (see p. 88) Reasoning Psychologist Helping Idiots Learn

- CHER – Chest, Hips, & Eyes Re-done!

- BAYWATCH – Beach Accidents Yield Wonderful Actresses To Chest Heaving

- TRUMP – Terrificly Rich, Ugly Megalomaniacal Power-trip

## What Should Be The Word Origin But Isn't:

An **acronym** is an acronym itself: Abbreviated Coded Rendition Of Name Yielding Meaning. The military created the term during World War II. Not true. But it should be! Also not true: the terms LOL, BRB, and TTYL were invented by U.S. generals as secret code to keep their communications' meanings hidden from the Russians. Of note: LOL, BRB, and TTYL are not technically acronyms because they don't create a word.

Tales of **yo momma's** reasonable age, weight, and appearance are **apocryphal**.

**a•poc•ry•phal** (uh POCK ri full)
adj. Inauthentic; of doubtful authority

According to legend, singer Phil Collins had a close friend who drowned. As the story goes, Collins wasn't close enough to help. One guy was, but did nothing. Collins wrote the song "In the Air Tonight," which indicts the anonymous man. He sent the man a ticket to a show, and shone a spotlight on him when he debuted the song. If you're a little **incredulous** (see p. 10) right now, we don't blame you: Odds are this one is completely false. Unless you know Phil Collins and can ask him, or were at the concert and can verify or disprove it, this is an example of an **apocryphal** story. Usually, apocryphal things have an element of being unable to be proved, such as an old war story, or the time you fended off an attack from eight ninjas with nothing but a rusty old menorah. Every trip to the mountains breeds the obligatory apocryphal fishing fable. And if you're wondering what **obligatory** means, it's your lucky day....

**ob•lig•a•tor•y** (uhb LIG uh tohr ee)
adj. Part of a very familiar routine, expected by all; mandatory, binding

Turkey and dressing are **obligatory** Thanksgiving dinner menu items. You utter obligatory in-case-I-crash I love yous to your loved ones before a long flight. Sitcoms have the obligatory wacky neighbor, and every *Star Trek* alien has the obligatory forehead deformity. Reality contest shows now have the obligatory British judge, an overused conceit which has resulted in a predictable **banality** (see p. 56).

## Yo momma is so old, ladybugs are shipped in large boxes of pinecones!

Aw snap…. Wait… what?  There's no word in the above entry because the sentence itself is an example of a **non sequitur** (nahn SEK wit uhr or -oor), a Latin phrase that has come, **verbatim**, into English. Non sequitur means "it doesn't follow." (Verbatim means "word for word," and is pronounced vuhr BAY tim.)  That ladybugs are shipped inside pinecone-filled boxes so they won't die in transit is a compelling factoid, but it has absolutely nothing to do with yo momma's advancing age.  So the phrase about ladybugs is a non sequitur.  It does not follow.  On *The Simpsons*, Ralph Wiggum's remarks show the humor that resides in a good non sequitur:

> Ralph: That's my swingset, and that's my sandbox. I'm not allowed to go in the deep end. And this is where I met the leprechaun.
> Bart: Right, the leprechaun.
> Ralph: He told me to burn things.

**Other Latin phrases/words:**

> **post hoc** (POST HOK) (Latin "after this")
> adj. & adv. Done after the fact

Russell Crowe hit a hotel desk attendant with a phone in New York and gave a weak post hoc justification on a bunch of talk shows.  **Ad hoc**, literally "to this," means done in the moment for a specific purpose.  Ad hoc committees are formed to handle issues that suddenly come up.  When rappers freestyle, that's ad hoc rhyming.

**quid pro quo** (KWID PRO KWOH)
Latin "what for what" or "this for that"
n. Something given in exchange for something else

George Clooney seems to have entered a **quid pro quo** arrangement with the movie studios, alternating between acting in commercial blockbusters (e.g. the *Ocean's* series) and making riskier but professionally rewarding fare such as *Good Night and Good Luck*.

**i.e.** (Please don't tell us you want a pronunciation key for two letters!)
Abbreviation meaning "that is, that is to say"

So you're reading something and encounter a parenthetical. You know, like this: "The Pittsburgh Steelers (i.e. the reigning Super Bowl champs) didn't make the playoffs." So you know that the abbreviation **"i.e."** explains something, but do you know exactly what it means? The abbreviation "i.e." stands for **id est**, a Latin phrase that means "that is." What you probably intuited about it is right: It serves to explain what precedes it, or to say it differently (i.e. in an alternative way). Got it? Now, onto i.e.'s cousin, **e.g.**, which is equally common.

Public figures (e.g. actors, politicians, singers) seem to need people's attention and adoration in almost any form (e.g. name-calling, fan mail, quoting the figures' own words at 3 A.M. to their windows). The abbreviation "e.g." means "for example." It comes from the Latin phrase **exempli gratia**, which means, literally, "for the sake of example." It's sort of like shorthand. It means the exact same thing as "for example," but it's several characters shorter and can be typed more quickly. Is there a better reason to pick up a word?

**de facto** [di FAK toh] or [day FAK toh]
adv. In fact, actually
adj. Describes someone or something that exists in fact

**De facto** is often used to document actual, though not titular, leadership. As in, "Many claim that Vice President Dick Cheney is the de facto leader of George W. Bush's administration," or "In *Grease*, Danny is the de facto leader of the T-Birds, the de facto social arbiters of Rydell High School." They aren't in any sense official leaders, but in practice and in fact they are. That's the adjectival definition. Adverbial usage documents the same idea, but (as adverbs do) describes an action: "Since Danny and Sandy are grounded and can't see each other, their parents de facto orchestrated a breakup." The spirit of de facto is that something is for real, though probably not determined via any official channels (i.e. Danny and Sandy weren't the parties that decided to break up, as they should have been, but nonetheless they're split).

## Quizzle

**Legal term or professional boxer?**

- Nolo Contendre
- Macho Camacho
- Res Ipso Loquitur
- Vitali Klitschko

*Answers: Macho Camacho and Vitali Klitschko are boxers.*

**Yo momma** is so ugly, the Rice Krispies **onomatopoeias** won't even talk to her!

**on·o·mat·o·poe·ia** (ahn uh maht uh PEE uh)
n. A word that imitates the sound it describes

The Rice Krispies elves Snap, Crackle, and Pop are **onomatopoeias**. Their names are words that sound like the noise they describe. Imagine a long line of wannabe Rice Krispies elfin mascots with **onomatopoetic** names at an audition: Chomp, Fizzle, Crunch, Splatter, Thwack, Twang, Whimper, Buzz, Murmur, etc. The old-school *Batman* television show was famous for using, and sometimes inventing, onomatopoeias and flashing them on the screen in cartoonish writing when punches were thrown.

**Onomatopoeias rejected by *Batman*:**

- Plon!
- Fworp!
- Bilf!
- Schweps!
- Utz!
- Asner!
- Shcmp
- Sffrt!
- Strep!
- Dwax!
- Whoomp!
- Bromgo!

**Vowels rejected by the word onomatopoeia:**

- "u"
- sometimes "y"

*Word to Your Mother!*

When writing the word **onomatopoeia**, you might as well just type a whole bunch of vowels really fast and hope the spell check fixes it for you.

# Yo daddy's so **epicene**, people confuse him with **yo momma**!

**ep·i·cene** (EP uh seen)

    adj. Sexless, but leaning toward the effeminate; having both (or neither) male and female characteristics, neuter

    n. An epicene person; with language, an epicene word

Do you know any "metrosexuals"? They're men who like women, and who, like women, are nonetheless concerned with their own grooming and appearance. They get eyebrow waxes and manicures, and spend bucks deluxe on spas, clothes and cosmetics. **Epicene** is the perfect word for metrosexuals. That is, metrosexuals aren't necessarily effeminate, but they might be described as just as effeminate as they are masculine. Calvin Klein released an epicene fragrance, cKone, which could be used by both men and women.

**Epicene or not? You decide.**

- Ryan Seacrest
- Dennis Rodman
- Colin Farrell
- Mike Tyson

- Robert Downey, Jr.
- Charlie Chaplin
- SpongeBob Squarepants
- Mike Tyson's voice

## *Word to Your Mother!*

**Epicene** has entered more common usage via linguistic discussions: Its most literal usage describes words that apply to both genders, usually pronouns. "We," for example, can apply to men and women alike (and is thus epicene); "he" and "she" cannot. Purists want an epicene pronoun to avoid using "he or she" or an inclusive "he," because it's cumbersome to say things like "Everyone put on his or her spandex."

Match the super power descriptions with the corresponding superhero.

**Powers:**

a) Nothing original about this hero. He wears a generic cape, fights crime, unloads on some bad guys... Blah Blah Blah... Boring!

b) This hero's battle cries include: "You are the most talented super-villain I've ever fought!" and "That spandex looks really flattering on you!"

c) Defeats his foes by pushing them out of windows. His one weakness: basements!

d) Sometimes he's a good guy; sometimes he's a bad guy. He can't decide on a costume either. He never seems to commit to anything!

**Heroes:**

- Blandish-Man (see **blandishments**, p. 126)
- Doctor Defenestration
- The **Fickle** Falcon (see p. 123)
- The Banal Baron

*Answers:* a) *The Banal Baron* b) *Blandish-Man* c) *Doctor Defenestration* d) *The Fickle Falcon*

**Yo momma** leaves such an **indelible** impression, when she gets into a dress, you can't even get her out with bleach! SNAP!

**in·del·i·ble** (in DELL uh buhl)
adj. Unable to be removed or erased

Late night infomercials pay washed-up celebrities to tell us about amazing cleaning products that can supposedly remove **indelible** stains from your carpet, upholstery or clothing. Indelible does not always describe an actual physical mark or stain. Martin Luther King's "I Have a Dream" speech left an indelible impression on millions of American listeners. Then again, so did that "Where's the Beef?" commercial. When you just can't get, say, the chorus to "Whoomp, There It Is" out of your head, it is **indelibly** imprinted in your brain. Tattoos are no longer indelible, as new laser technology can remove them. Since the removal process is so expensive and painful, however, tattoos are **de facto** (see p. 98) indelible. So think before you ink!

**Ten indelible tattoos you might regret:**

- The Chinese symbol for "need for attention"
- Periodic table across chest
- Simulated tuft of lower back hair
- Squashed bug on bottom of foot
- Scratch and Sniff pickle tattoo
- The Chinese symbol for "trite"
- MAD Magazine-style "fold-in" using stomach folds
- Growth chart of inch marks up entire body
- Portraits of U.S. vice presidents all over body
- Fake tuxedo
- Bruise
- Varicose vein illusion

# The World's Worst Yo Momma Jokes

**Yo momma** is so fat that it makes her prone to adult onset diabetes, significantly raising the risk of coronary heart disease and stroke.

**Yo momma** is so stupid due to a lack of accessibility to decent educational institutions for those in lower income brackets, she has to work low-paying, menial jobs, which in turn strips her children of decent educational opportunities, perpetuating a vicious cycle of socio-economic stagnancy.

**Yo momma** is so ugly she is unable to attract a mate, thereby ending her genetic legacy and leaving her psychologically and spiritually unfulfilled.

**Yo momma's** breath so stank because of a genetic defect that produces chronic halitosis. Her problem could be symptomatic of a far graver illness.

**Yo momma's** so old, she has become a burden on her family, demanding their time and energy, both of which could be better utilized personally and professionally.

## Quizzle

The author of the snaps listed above doesn't quite get the game. He is _____ when it comes to catching on to the _____ of **Yo Momma** battles, instead weighing down his snaps with unwarranted _____ .

   a) effusive, cacophony, harridans

   b) prostrate, vestiges, equanimity

   c) obtuse, persiflage, gravitas

   d) swollen, sampleton, Luis Guzmans

*Answer: c*

# Yo momma is **cathartic**. I saw her and I threw up!

Don't assume that **cathartic** means ugly here. Remember, when you "assume," you make an "assu" out of "me." Wait, that's not right. Anyway, the actual definition of cathartic is as follows:

**ca·thar·tic** (cuh THAR tik)
adj. Giving relief by motivating a purge of some sort, usually emotional

A **catharsis** is a moment of emotional purging, a sometimes violent emptying of anger, sadness, distress, etc. **Cathartic** moments are generally considered to be psychologically healthy and even necessary. If you've been bottling up your emotions and then something finally sets you off and you sob uncontrollably, you are having a catharsis. Art can have a cathartic effect on people. By living **vicariously** (see p. 60) through the characters in movies, for example, we can relieve ourselves of emotional tension.

## No Wrong Answers

Now that you know its meaning, "Catharsis" is...

A good name for a child (Cathy for short)?

A good name for a punk band?

A good name for an energy drink?

A good name for a car model?

A good name for a restaurant?

A good name for a bar?

A good name for a mouthwash?

**Yo momma** has such **pathos**, I took one look at her face and cried for days!

**pa·thos** (PAY thoss) or (Pay thohs)
n. A quality that evokes sorrow or pity; sympathetic pity

Serious artists hope their work has **pathos**. Actors play the roles of increasingly disabled characters hoping that their portrayal of, say, a paraplegic, dyslexic, autistic rodeo clown exhibits pathos worthy of an Oscar. However, if the portrayal is too heavy-handed, it may exhibit **bathos** (BAY thoss or BAY thohs)—excessive, insincere pathos, or **mawkishness** (see p. 84). If you have a friend or relative who's a creative type, but who lacks any real ability, pathos is a useful word to deploy. If you really hate your friend's stuff, you can say that his painting of a pheasant being blown to smithereens by birdshot "has such pathos": He'll think that you mean that its pathos resides in a deep empathy for the sadness inherent in the hunt, whereas to you, the pathos stems from the fact that this terrifically bad dead-bird painting exists at all.

**"Blues Songs" with little pathos:**

- "I Didn't Get Into Harvard (But I Did Get Into Brown, My Safety School)"

- "Grass Stains Ain't Coming Out"

- "What Is With This Airplane Food, Anyway?"

- "My Beret Is Askew"

- "Drowning My Sorrows in Zima"

- "My Papillary Conjunctivitis Is Recurring (It Just Don't Go Away)"

- "I Can't Find The Afikoman (No Matter How Hard I Look)"

# Yo momma's gas is so **vehemently**

fetid (see p. 15), the National Weather Service assigns names to her "releases."

**ve•he•ment** (VEE uh ment)
adj. Forcefully intense; zealous, impassioned

Ever been in a movie theater when everyone spontaneously applauds because something so cool happened onscreen? That eruption, you and everybody else yelling at the screen and clapping, pumping your fists, exhibits **vehement** enthusiasm. So now you can understand the severity of yo momma's aforementioned problem. Vehement is often used to express support or opposition: Rumsfeld **vehemently** defended his position regarding Iraq; somebody else vehemently opposed it; and on and on. A similar word is **emphatic**, which also means forceful and intense, but often applies to something said or performed: When Lupé asked Pedro if he wanted to go to the magic convention, Pedro responded with an emphatic yes. (And who wouldn't when offered to go with Lupé to the magic convention?!) By the way, since this a PG-13 book, we chose to use the **euphemism** "releases" in our snap.

**eu•phe•mism** (YOO fuh mizm)
n. An inoffensive substitution for a term that is offensive, blunt or vulgar

We use **euphemisms** when speaking or writing to soften the blow. Examples of euphemisms are "not the sharpest tool in the shed" for "stupid" and "downsize" for the more blunt "fire everyone." If yo momma were creating an online dating profile, we might describe her build **euphemistically** as "athletic."

# Yo beautiful momma is an oxymoron!

**ox·y·mor·on** (ahks ee MOHR ahn)
n. A figure of speech that describes the combination of two contradictory terms

Wait, that's not a compliment. To be vaguely precise about **oxymora** (that's a correct plural form, as is **oxymorons**): They're rightly wrong, but, if used correctly, can be awfully nice. Usually an **oxymoron** will take the form of an adjective-noun combination, such as "boring entertainment," "deafening silence," or "intelligent beach reading." But that's not the only way—we use adverb-adjective combos above, and there are adjective-adjective combos such as "bittersweet" and "little big." The key to oxymorons is that they *make sense*. They are not errors in usage. If you're a new attorney and you find yourself arguing a case in front of the Supreme Court, what better way to document your emotions than to say you stepped before the court with "meek confidence"? Or that, when they began to question you and your nervousness kicked in, your pants became "warmly cold"?

## Quizzle

**Which of the following oxymorons are real musicians?**

a) Biggie Smalls

b) Jumbo Shrimp

c) Fatboy Slim

d) Compassionate Conservative

*Answers: a and c are real*

## Word to Your Mother!

For a killer lively list of **oxymorons**, check out www.oxymoronlist.com.

# Yo momma is so **porcine**, when I asked for pigs in a blanket, she got back in bed.

**por·cine** (POR sign)

adj. Of or resembling a pig

Almost every animal has a corresponding adjective that means "of or resembling a (insert animal)." We all know canine (dog) and feline (cat), but there are also: **bovine** (cow); **vulpine** (fox); **lupine** (wolf); **ursine** (bear) **murine** (rat); **bubaline** (buffalo); and countless others. Some of these words have meanings that then extend from the literal. **Porcine** can mean piggish in features or repulsively overweight. Vulpine can mean cunning. Bovine can mean sluggish. Animal words such as these can effectively evoke imagery when describing people's appearance or behavior.

**Sampling:**

*Chris Farley's* **ursine** *bulk* belied *(contradicted) a* **vulpine** *mind and an agility that was more* **feline** *than* **bovine**.

## Quizzle

Match the animal with the term that describes it.

- lion
- wasp
- eagle
- sheep
- bull
- Former NBA great Ralph Sampson

- vespine
- ovine
- sampsonine
- taurine
- leonine
- aquiline—can also mean "curved down and hooked"

*Answers: lion (leonine); wasp (vespine); eagle (aquiline); sheep (ovine); bull (taurine); Sampson (sampsonine)*

# Yo momma's wardrobe is so **exiguous**,
## it makes a homeless person's look **copious**.

**ex·i·gu·ous** (ig ZIG yoo us)
adj. Meager, inadequate

There's more than one reason why yo momma's wardrobe might be **exiguous**: Yo momma may be so **corpulent** (see p. 4) and **Brobdingnagian** (see p. 8) that almost no clothes fit her, so things she's able to wear are very few in number. Second, we've established how poor yo momma is, so she also can't buy any clothes. Imagine her closet, with one or two lonely, **amorphous** (see p. 44) dresses that look like tents or parachutes hanging on a couple of hangers, probably all the way down to the floor. Man, yo momma's got it bad. There was a degree of **exiguousness** to the life lived by Leonardo DiCaprio's character in *Titanic*, who was so poor he had to sneak onto the ship. Then he fell in love with Kate Winslet and his love life became anything but exiguous. Until he died.

**co·pi·ous** (COH pee us)
adj. Plentiful, large in quantity or number

You've heard this word, usually pertaining to food. "A **copious** harvest" is a very common phrase, as in "Yo momma's harvest was so copious, the bountiful crop wasn't just around the house, it was AROUND the house." Another example: "At the wedding, the buffet was so copious, it looked as if nobody was eating." Or: "The Taco Bell kitchen is so copious, yo momma never gets bored." Copious doesn't have to apply to food, however: "The copious resources of George Steinbrenner allow him to snare the best baseball players, making the Yankees perennial contenders."

**Sampling:**

*There are **copious** examples of usages of the word "**copious**" in the preceding paragraph, so this one borders on being **superfluous** (see p. 86).*

Match the super power descriptions with the corresponding superhero.

**Powers:**

a) Brings his foes to tears by showing them overly sentimental home movies of their childhood. Carries an assortment of sappy greeting cards on his utility belt.

b) Powers include: "Deafening silence," "Controlled chaos," "Growing smaller," and being "Cautiously optimistic."

c) Fights crime underwater as long as you agree to do him an equal favor in return.

d) The 5th member of "The Fantastic Four" who was released from his contract.

e) Wages battle against anyone who isn't from her native country.

**Heroes:**

- The Mawkish Marvel
- Squid Pro Quo
- Super Fluous
- Xenophobia Warrior Princess
- The Oxymoron

*Answers: a) The Mawkish Marvel; b) The Oxymoron; c) Squid Pro Quo; d) Super Fluous; e) Xenophobia Warrior Princess*

# **Yo momma** is so **acrophobic**, she fainted when she stepped onto the curb!

**acrophobic** (ak ruh FOH bik)
adj. Afraid of heights

That's a low blow. Which is a good thing for yo momma, because she's afraid of heights. If yo momma is wary of such a short height (**oxymoron**, see p. 107), she suffers from ridiculously serious (oxymoron again) **acrophobia**. She needs to crouch down when she walks, she's so **acrophobic**. She drives a low-rider and lives in a low-rise building. **Phobias** are pathological fears, and human beings, rough draft of species that they are, have all kinds of them. There is a psychological term for just about every fear you can think of. By the way, don't mistake acrophobia with **arachnophobia** (fear of spiders), which was, of course, the title of a thrilling movie.

**Which of these phobias would make the worst movie?**

**Atychiphobia** *Fear of failure*
The daughter of a senator has been kidnapped, and forensic psychologist Alex Crow is the only man who can unravel the clues that can save her. But since there is a chance it might not work, he does nothing, and she is never recovered.

**Dextrophobia** *Fear of objects at the right side of the body*
Mundy Tate has spent his entire life looking to the left. But when people keep referring to him as "you guys," Mundy must face the fact that he has a Siamese twin.

**Hippopotomonstrosesquippedaliophobia**
*Fear of long words*
A woman suffering from hippopotomonstrosesquippedaliophobia discovers that there is no fear greater than the fear of being afraid of the name of the fear that you are afraid of.

**Hexakosioihexekontahexaphobia** *Fear of the number 666*
$(458/4) - (45.5+506) = $ TERROR!

## What Has Yo Momma Taught You So Far?

Match the character with the appropriate quote.

1. The Sanguine Pirate
2. The Grandiloquent Bowling Shop Attendant
3. The Timorous Milkman
4. The Laconic Robot
5. The Moribund Ringmaster
6. The Agnostic Football Star
7. The Ambivalent Cliff Diver

a) "Ladies and gentleman, children of all…ahhhhhhhhhhhhhh…" (crumples to ground).

b) "I'm sure we'll see land soon, and we'll get through this scurvy. I know we will. Call me an optimist, but fate is not ARRRRRRRRRbitrary!"

c) "I just want to thank the guy above, if he does in fact exist, for giving me the strength to score that touchdown. If not, let me thank the process of evolution for giving me the opposable digits with which to catch the ball."

d) "Permit me to return with the utmost expediency the spheroid with which you will **prostrate** (see p. 8) the pins."

e) "Kill all humans."

f) "Oh, er… um… (hands shake)… here's your 2%… um… if you want… I mean, good day now."

g) "Water looks rough. Then again, I love the exhilaration. Wind is unpredictable though. And yet, if I time it right, I might be okay."

*Answers: 1b; 2d; 3f; 4e; 5a; 6c; 7g*

# Yo momma's so **sedentary**, she's got a
remote control to operate her remote!

**sed·en·tar·y** (SED n tare ee)
adj. Characterized by sitting or being inactive

A **sedentary** lifestyle is one that requires or exhibits little or no exercise. Yo momma is like most Americans, whose sedentary lifestyle has resulted in **superfluous** (see p. 86) flab and common **corpulence** (see p. 4). An **advocate** (see p. 67) of the sedentary lifestyle is Homer Simpson. In one episode of *The Simpsons*, Homer uses his "typing wand" to push buttons on his computer keyboard from the couch. In another episode, Homer becomes the **apotheosis** ( see p. 85) of **sedentariness** when he invents the "toilet chair," **obviating** (or making unnecessary) the need to get up. If your couch has a permanent indentation of your lower half, it is likely a sign of a sedentary life.

**The Ultimate Sedentary Day Planner:**

1:00 P.M.  Get up (i.e. move from lying position to sitting)

2:00 P.M.  Eat from "pillow trough" of food

3:00 P.M.  Put on adult diaper

4:00 P.M.  Search crevices of sofa-bed for stranded food bits

5:00 P.M.  TV

6:00 P.M.  Use adult diaper

7:00 P.M.  Order pizza (have them put it in bucket attached to string)

10:00 P.M.  Video games (*Seated Warrior*, *Sim Sit*, *Revenge of Stephen Hawking*)

11:00 P.M.  Bed

Match the character with the appropriate quote.

**1.** The Megalomaniacal Bellboy

**2.** The Incredulous Foot Locker Salesman

**3.** The Effusive Busboy

**4.** The Sorcerer Who Lives Vicariously Through His Son

**5.** The Taciturn Window Washer

**6.** The Captious Leprechaun

a) Oh my gosh, thank you sooooooo much for eating here! Let me just get that salad plate! That shirt is so nice! I would love, absolutely love, to top off that water for you!

b) No way do you wear a wide. Are you serious?

c) The purple in that rainbow is slightly dull. And look where this gold has been placed, at least three inches to the right of the base! Come on!

d) (Silence.)

e) My boy recently was in a battle against a chromatic dragon. He cast two fireball spells. Two! It was great! You could feel the heat of the dragon breath!

f) Let me grab your bag, Sir. And then you will see I am the greatest luggage carrier in the history of mankind! The minstrels will forever sing of my greatness.

*Answers: 1f; 2b; 3a; 4e; 5d; 6c*

# Yo Momma's Interlude of Exposition

**ex·po·si·tion** (eks puh ZISH n)
n. Detailed explanation

**Exposition** has a number of definitions, the simplest and broadest of which is "a detailed explanation." In a movie, when someone sums up relevant prior events so the audience can follow what's happening, that's exposition. This paragraph is exposition of what exposition means. Sometimes, you can have too much exposition, too much detail in your explanation, and you end up taking the wind out of your sails.

**Observational Comedy With Too Much Exposition:**

What is with airplane crashes? If the only thing that survives the plane crash is the black box, why don't they build the whole plane of that black box? Likely, it is because the material wouldn't withstand the rigors of flight, is too expensive and heavy to use in large scale, and it's more a matter of shape and construction than it is a matter of material.

And what's with the age-gap hiring policy at most movie theaters? Didja ever notice they never hire anyone between 15 and 80? Know what I mean? It must have something to do with the sad way old people are treated in this country, increasingly marginalized into obsolescence by new technology.

Would somebody please explain to me those signs that say, "No animals allowed except for Seeing Eye Dogs?" Who is this sign for? I suppose it is for the many non-sight impaired people accompanying blind people as well as those who were considering bringing an animal on the premises. Do the math.

# Yo momma's so **execrable**, her family planned her funeral with **alacrity**.

**ex·e·cra·ble** (EKS uh cruh bul)
adj. Detestable, abominable

If something, someone, or yo momma is **execrable**, it/he/she/yo momma is hated, detested even, and deserving of all of it. The more common words are fine, but execrable will do the trick: The show *Date My Mom* on MTV is an execrable act against humanity. The verb **execrate**, meaning to detest, can do the same thing, and if someone hurls **execration** at yo momma, he's telling her that he loathes her very much.

**a·lac·ri·ty** (uh LAK ri tee)
n. Cheerful promptness

Things that you do with **alacrity** you do happily and without delay. You RSVP to parties that you're psyched about attending with alacrity. You deposit checks with alacrity (if they're made out to you). After Jennifer Aniston, Brad Pitt hopped into Angelina Jolie's waiting arms with alacrity, and they made a family, complete with children and trips to the subcontinent, with **alacritous** abandon.

## *Word to Your Mother!*

We would love to report that the Pitt-Jolie union happened **alacritously**, but that would be incorrect usage: There's no adverbial form of this word. That is, people can't do things alacritously; they must do them with **alacrity**.

# Isn't **Yo Momma** Ironic?

Perhaps you remember one of the more genius tunes ever to travel the radio waves: "Ironic," a 1995 hit by Alanis Morissette. The tune is brilliant because it's **ironic** itself: None of the things in the song that Morissette describes as ironic are actually ironic. Ah, the **irony**! So let's explain what irony is. Irony (which is what Morissette attempts to document) occurs when something happens contrary to what you expected, and the result is usually a little amusing to somebody. The song "Ironic" says that "rain on your wedding day" is ironic. Not necessarily. What would be ironic is if the wedding had been held in the desert specifically to avoid the rain, and it had rained. Dr. Atkins, who hatched the low-carb diet that bears his name, died of a heart attack. That's ironic.

**Yo Momma's other misuses:**
Never say **irregardless**. It's not a word. Both the prefix "ir-" and the suffix "-less" are negatives, so they cancel each other out. Use "regardless" and stop being a **cretin** (CREET n), or a stupid person.

If you're scared of something, this does not mean that you're **mortified**. Being mortified indicates a degree of shameful embarrassment.

We're almost done, before you get **nauseated** with this list of correct usage. If this list were 60 pages long and in a 4-point font, it might well be classified as **nauseous**. That is, it's disgusting to think about—not sick to its stomach. If you might vomit, you're nauseated. Careful if you describe yourself as "nauseous," which technically means that you make others nauseated. However, at some point when people misuse a word so often, the "incorrect" usage can become "correct" usage, a phenomenon that word nerds and grammar gestapos find, well, nauseous.

**Yo momma's** car's so **dilapidated**, someone broke in just to steal The Club.

**di·lap·i·dat·ed** (dih LAP ih date id)
adj. Run-down, in a poor condition, usually as a result of insufficient care

**Dilapidated** means run-down and shoddy. That which is dilapidated was once functional, perhaps even impressive, but has fallen into a state of ruin or decay. So if yo momma's Ford Taurus has become dilapidated, it has lost its former glory and is now ready for the junkyard. In some rural areas, you drive by dilapidated wooden shacks and barns, structures that are so rotten and **askew** (see p. 75), a stiff wind could knock them over. Abandoned buildings can be dilapidated. An old dock worn down by the tides might be dilapidated. As we get older, our bodies become dilapidated, until we become the guy on the basketball court "just trying to get a little exercise."

**Yo momma** maintains such **equanimity**, she makes Lace Placid look volatile!

**e·qua·nim·i·ty** (ee kwa NIHM i tee or ek wa)
n. Composure (especially under pressure)

The trick for people in the public eye is to cultivate a reputation for being able to maintain their **equanimity**. Witness what happened to Howard Dean, the onetime frontrunner for the 2004 Democratic presidential nomination, when he emitted a gleeful shriek after a third-place finish in Iowa. Television shows played "the scream" again and again, and he was out of the race. Or Tom Cruise, who, despite being one of the biggest-grossing movie stars of all time, was dropped unceremoniously by Paramount after jumping on Oprah Winfrey's couch and **castigating** (see p. 90) Matt Lauer on *The Today Show*. He lost his equanimity, and his publicist couldn't seem to find it.

Complete the name of the reality TV show with the word that best fits the show's description.

Words: esophoric, charlatan, indelible, fetid, askew, timorous

**1.** *America's Most _____ Home Videos*
Clips from this show include: "Cinematographer has one leg shorter than the other" and "Baby filmed by camera on an uneven tripod."

**2.** *The World's Most _____ Police Chases*
The cops nervously keep a safe distance while pursuing a 90-year-old woman in a Buick. When she suddenly signals a left turn, the police surrender.

**3.** *Girls Gone _____*
Cross-eyed college coeds pose for the camera while on Spring Break.

**4.** *America's Next Top _____*
16 girls cheat and lie in hopes of fooling people into thinking that they are fake supermodels.

**5.** *_____ Makeover*
Women have their makeup changed. Hopefully they like it, because it's permanent!

**6.** *Lifestyles of the Rich and _____*
On this episode, a billionaire media mogul explains why he hasn't showered in six years and why he refuses to use deodorant.

*Answers: 1. askew; 2. timorous; 3. esophoric; 4. charlatan; 5. indelible; 6. fetid*

# Yo Momma's "Almost Human"

**anthropomorphism**
(an thruh puh MORF izm)
> n. The act of ascribing human traits to non-human creatures or things

**Anthropomorphism** is a long, **sesquipedalian** (see p. 12) word, but it's a good one. We **anthropomorphize** our pets all the time, speaking to them as if they were human. When animated movies humanize animals, objects, or any other non-human creatures or things, they are **anthropomorphizing** them. Pixar, the can-do-no-wrong purveyor of kids' films, has made **anthropomorphic** stories about toys, cars, and bugs, to name a few. But not every anthropomorphic tale is appropriate for kids.

**Rejected Pixar films featuring anthropormorphism:**

*Nooks and Crannies* - A neurotic English muffin and a bipolar stick of butter quest for freedom in an Indianapolis diner.

*Roadkill* - Zombie movie in which bloody pulps and carcasses pry themselves from the road, rising from the dead to avenge their deaths; *Kill Bill* in tone.

*Finding Nemo 2* - Nemo is caught, broiled, eaten and digested; Bernie Mac attached as voice of the pancreas.

*Opposites Detract* - A dog and a cat switch bodies. Neither survives the process and both die in minutes; short film.

*Kankers* - Musical with Carol Channing as the leader of a band of lovable lip sores that try to help their host fall in love.

# Yo momma's so fat, diets are **anathema** to her.

**a·nath·e·ma** (un NATH em uh)
n. Something banned or denounced; something utterly detested

To understand fully what **anathema** means, picture Tony Soprano or one of his mobster crew saying about someone who has betrayed them, "He's dead to me": It means the same thing. Anathema, of course, doesn't mean "dead"; it's more of a ban, an absolute denunciation. If something's anathema, you have nothing to do with it. It's likely that Angelina Jolie's name is anathema in the Jennifer Aniston household. In common usage, anathema takes on the second definition, or "something loathed": "DJ's with **askew** (see p. 75) visors are anathema to me" or "Cell phone rings are anathema to movie audiences." If diets truly are anathema to yo momma, then it's possible that:

# Yo momma's so rapidly **burgeoning**, they need to measure her growth with aerial photographs!

**bur·geon** (BUR juhn)
v. To develop or increase quickly, flourish

Google's **burgeoning ubiquity** (see p. 121 and p. 1) is inarguable: Everybody uses it every day. The company is taking over the world. The burgeoning popularity of video on the Web enabled YouTube to sell out to Google for over $1 billion after less than two years of allowing people to post videos of themselves pouring tea, falling off a roof, or lip-synching poorly. When something **burgeons**, it experiences noticeable and quick expansion or development. Snowboarding has **burgeoned** as a recreation activity in recent years, even becoming an Olympic event. Your vocabulary is burgeoning with each snap you read, natch.

**Yo momma** is so dumb, she thought Taco Bell was a Mex— By the way, have you had the Taco Bell chorizo fajita? It's great. They have like this pepper jack cheese sauce, but I **digress**…

**di·gress** (die GRESS)
v. To wander off topic when speaking or writing

To **digress** is to deviate from the main subject when you are talking or writing. If you want to see an example of a **digression**, check out the **parasite** entry in this book (see p. 122). Children's speech is often composed of one digression after another—"Can we get the movie? I like TV better than movies. I like the Wiggles!"—until the main subject can no longer be remembered, and the digressions border on **non sequiturs** (see p. 96): "I want juice. Yellow is my favorite color. I have a friend robot." A closely related word is **tangent**. If you go off on a tangent, it means you suddenly digress.

**Sampling:**

*The blind date was officially **moribund** (see p. 139) when Merle went into a 15-minute **digression** on the reasons Romulans were superior to Klingons.*

**Yo momma** is so **ethereal**, she falls UP the stairs!

**e·the·re·al** (i THEER ee uhl)
adj. Light, delicate, otherworldly

Yo momma is light, not thin or **emaciated** (see p. 1), but light and airy. Yo momma is like a feather, a vapor, like light. Yo momma, dare we admit it, is almost heavenly, another meaning of **ethereal**. Yo momma is practically **intangible** or **impalpable**, both of which mean incapable of being touched.

# Yo momma is so **mercurial**, her mood ring is a strobe light!

**mer·cur·i·al** (mer KYOOR ee uhl)
adj. Subject to volatile changes

Yo momma is cool and relaxed one moment, then suddenly angry and wrathful. She's composed and confident one day, and a wreck the next. Hence her strobing mood ring. With her **mercurial** moods, yo momma can also be described as having a temperament that is **fickle** (constantly changing). The career of John Travolta, from *Saturday Night Fever* stardom, to *Perfect* obscurity, to a *Pulp Fiction* resurgence is nothing if not mercurial. Mercurial has a second meaning: having traits attributed to the god Mercury (eloquence, shrewdness, swiftness), and can also mean "spirited," so you can simultaneously insult and compliment someone with this word.

**Sampling:**

*Deandre's hair had a **mercurial** temperament, lying flat and behaved one day, and defying gravity the next.*

# Yo momma is such a **martinet**, she made you do 50 pushups before she would give birth to you.

**mar·ti·net** (mart NET)
n. A firm disciplinarian

**Martinetish** parents get lambasted on TV and in the movies all the time. Coaches are often **martinets**. Consider the stereotypical hiked-up shorts wearing, **vociferous** (see p. 28) high school football coach who makes his players run thirty laps if they're one minute late for practice. There's a whiff of the military in "martinet," and that's because of the word's origin (see p. 32).

## Better Words For Yo Momma

**Yo momma** is so **incorrigibly** stupid, she moves her lips when listening to an audio tape.

**in·cor·ri·gi·ble** (in CORE rij ih bul)
adj. Beyond reform, unable to be corrected

It's hopeless. Yo momma cannot be helped. Her behavior, and in the case above, her stupidity, cannot be corrected, nor even **ameliorated** (made better) and is therefore **incorrigible**. Incorrigible is the better word for the clumsy "uncorrectable."

**Yo momma's** appetite is so **insatiable**, she eats muffins like tic tacs!

**in·sa·tia·ble** (in SAY shuh bul)
adj. Unable to be satisfied

If yo momma has an **insatiable** appetite, it cannot be satisfied or **satiated**. Insatiable is the real word that exists for the clumsy non-word "unsatisfiable." It is similar to **voracious** (see p. 3), but even stronger, as insatiable indicates a desire that can never be satisfied.

**Yo momma** is so **inexplicably** clumsy, she could trip over a cordless phone.

**in·ex·plic·a·ble** (in eks PLIK uh bul)
adj. Unable to be explained

**Inexplicable** things are difficult if not impossible to account for. They are mystifying. The **ephemeral** (see p. 17) popularity of Billy Ray Cyrus was inexplicable. Use "inexplicable" when you would use the imprecise and clumsy "unexplainable" to mean mystifying or impossible to understand.

**Yo momma's** so **obsequious**, she pulled up
at the Holland Tunnel and tried to pay a
compliment!  Oh, no you di'n't!  Snap!

**ob·se·qui·ous** (ahb SEE kwee us)
adj.  Excessively servile

Most people find it convenient simply to pay the $6 in cash to
bid good riddance to the Garden State.  But not your mother.
**Obsequious** people seek nothing more than to advance their
way in the world through shotgun sprays of **copious** (see p. 109)
praise.  The key with **obsequiousness** is the calculated self-
interest.  If you are obsequious, you are a **sycophant**.  They say
that beside every great man there is a woman.  And vice versa.
But behind both of them is a staff of sniveling sycophants.

**Sampling:**

> *The Hollywood assistant was always armed with* **obsequious**
> *praise and a bottle of water to offer guests.*

**Yo momma's** so ugly, looking at her face
**annealed** me.

**an·neal** (uh NEEL)
v.  To strengthen by hardship

Maybe you didn't make the football or volleyball team.  Maybe
you got dumped.  Maybe your parachute didn't open.  Whatever
the incident, you emerged from it tougher, the better for having
been through it.  Trying circumstances often **anneal** you.  In
metallurgy, heating a metal and then gradually cooling it in order
to improve its internal properties is called **annealing**.  The
ridiculous tasks assigned him by Mr. Miyagi ("Wax on!" "Wax
off!") **annealed** Ralph Macchio in *The Karate Kid*.  By *Karate
Kid 3*, however, Macchio had to start questioning the annealing
value of re-tarring Miyagi's driveway.

# Yo momma's so needy, she believes the blandishments of mountebanks! Snap!

**moun·te·bank** [MOUN ti bank] (MOUN is pronounced like the first syllable of "mountain")

> n. A self-promoting swindler, someone who defrauds others in a very public way

Note first that "**mountebank**" has three syllables. It's not pronounced MOUNT bank. Although they aren't always stealing, if they are, **mountebanks** are the most ego-driven of thieves: It's not enough for them to defraud people on the way to making money; they must do it while they have people's attention. Mountebanks differ from **charlatans** in that charlatans aren't necessarily trying to get money (although they sometimes do)—they're just presenting themselves as something they are not, and they do it arrogantly and loudly.

**bland·ish·ment** (BLAND ish ment)

> n. Flattery with the purpose of persuading

Car salesmen—or so the stereotype goes—tell people what they want to hear, and simultaneously convince you that you need more than you actually do. Part of the game is showering customers with **blandishments**: They **blandish** you, and create a bond that makes you not want to let them down. The thing with each blandishment is that it comes with a bit of self-interest: The salesmen, after all, make a living selling cars, and the pricier the better. (Note that a general, non-specific use of a flattering remark takes the plural—"blandishments," the more common usage—and that one flattering remark is a "**blandishment**.") By the way, you read this book so well. You should teach this stuff—and buy the necessary number of copies to do so.

**Yo momma** does things so **circuitously**, she takes 4 days to watch 48 hrs!

**cir·cu·i·tous** (sir KYOO i tuss)
adj. Indirect or roundabout

And she takes 48 hrs to watch *24*. And she watches Anderson Cooper 720. Wait, that last one doesn't work. How about, "Yo momma's so revolving she watches Anderson 720"? So dizzy? We'll work on it. Anyway, we **digress** (see p. 122). The etymology of this one isn't too much of a bear: It comes from the Latin word *circuitus*, which means, more or less, "a way around." Gender-stereotypical male-bashing driving usage: "Taking the **circuitous** route is better than stopping to ask directions." Gender-stereotypical female-bashing conversational usage: "Over 300 hours, Sally took a circuitous conversational journey toward asking Alphonso if they were in fact dating."

The prefix **circ-** means "round." The prefix **circum-** means "around." If you walk entirely around something, you've **circumambulated** it. If you **circumscribe** something, you draw around or encircle it. To stretch: "Yo momma is so **circumscribing**, when she sits around the house, she sits AROUND the house. Circumscribe can mean, more vaguely, "to mark off or delimit."

## Quizzle

Which are bogus words?

- **Circumspect** – Watchful, cautious, mindful of possible consequences
- **Circumvent** – To avoid or bypass (especially by strategic maneuvering)
- **Circumoblique** – Curved around so as not to intersect
- **Circumnavigate** – To proceed entirely around
- **Circumgarnish** – To encircle with parsley

*Answers: Circumoblique and circumgarnish are fake.*

# Yo Momma's Tasty Leftovers

## Yo momma's so **meticulous**, she keeps her date book in triplicate!

**me·tic·u·lous** (muh TIK yoo luss)
adj. Exact in the following of details

**Meticulous** mommas are mommas who adhere to every minute detail of some routine, process, or action. Yo momma might be meticulous about setting the table just right or organizing her files on her computer.

## Yo momma is so **jingoistic**, she got U.S. flag contact lenses.

**jin·go·is·tic** (jing oh ISS tik)
adj. Excessively patriotic, often accompanied by belligerent foreign policy

Professional wrestling fans often chant "USA! USA!" even if the villainous wrestler is a rather unthreatening Canadian. They want the American wrestler to tear apart the neighbor from the north. These fans are **jingoistic**.

## Yo momma put the "pig" in "**epigone**"!

**ep·i·gone** (EP uh gohn) (Note: last syllable rhymes with "bone")
n. A less talented imitator (or a less distinguished imitation) of someone or something

Examples of **epigones** are many: George W. Bush has been called an **epigone** of Ronald Reagan, Oasis of The Beatles.

# Yo momma's insidiously ugly: Her face is like a Magic Eye 3D picture that you have to stare at until you realize exactly how ugly she is!

**in·sid·i·ous** (in SIDD ee us)
adj. Stealthily harmful

"Debbie Downer," *Saturday Night Live's* resident doomsayer, discusses the **insidiousness** of mad cow disease when someone orders steak ("It can live in your body for years before it ravages your brain"). Something that is is harmful, but in a **surreptitious** (stealthy, difficult to detect) way. Some people claim Michael Moore's movies are full of insidious propaganda disguised as entertainment. Pollution is an insidious threat to the environment. *The Yo Momma Vocabulary Builder* is "insidiously educational."

# Yo momma is so gamine, she has to step into her shirts.

**gam·ine** (ga MEEN Note: "ga" sounds the same as in "gap")
n. A very slender, charmingly mischievous girl
adj. Of or like a gamine

The word "**gamine**" comes from the French "*gamin*" and originally was used to describe playful and mischievous **waifs** (homeless or helpless, uncared-for people, usually children). Nowadays, it's often associated with slender and desirable young women who wear disproportionately large designer sunglasses on their oversized lollipop-like heads. We're talking, of course, about Nicole Richie and the Olsen Twins, or any other fashionista who survives on a diet of sugar-free Red Bull and nicotine. But let us not forget Audrey Hepburn, the ever-so-popular president of the 1950's Lollipop Head Guild, who paved the way for future gamine greats like Kate Moss, Calista Flockhart and Ellen Pompeo.

# Yo momma is so **braggadocious**,
### she makes Muhammad Ali look unassuming!

**brag·ga·do·cious** (brag uh DOH shuhs)
adj. Overly boastful and proud

Lots of rappers are **braggadocious**, noisily boasting about how good they are at performing as they perform: "My oratory gift is abundant, so dazzling to mind that you should come get..." from "As I Read My S-A" by Gang Starr. More humble, less braggadocious musicians tend to let the music speak for itself: They don't need to proclaim **mellifluously** (see p. 25), "I am very skilled at playing this guitar and singing an accompanying tune." The exception is Barry Manilow, who **braggadociously** sings, "I write the songs that make the whole world sing." Barry's claim borders on **hubris** (excessive pride that often leads to one's downfall).

# You momma's so **introverted**, her only
### MySpace friend is herself!

**in•tro•vert** (IN truh vert)
adj. Someone who is shy and keeps to him or herself

If you're **introverted**, you look inward a lot. You like your alone time. You draw your energy from yourself as opposed to crowds. You monitor and examine your own thoughts with care and interest. Think Tiger Woods, the world's greatest golfer and a noted **introvert**. (He named his yacht "Privacy.")

## Yo Mnomma's Mnemonics:

*Introvert vs. Extrovert Skating*
*John is an **introverted** skater. He skates by himself, using the meditative experience of gliding down a halfpipe to aid in his feeling at peace with himself. Larry is an **extroverted** skater. He skates with lots of friends, enjoying their company, learning tricks from them.*

# Yo momma is so beset by **ennui**, she sighed to death! Aw, snap!

**en·nui** (ahn WEE)
   n. Extreme boredom and listlessness

**Ennui** is the kind of boredom that sinks into you and weighs you down. It has more permanent or long-lasting connotations than boredom. Throw in a tinge of melancholy, a hair of dissatisfaction and a dash of weariness, and you have one interesting variety of bored. This may be a difficult concept to grasp. Give it ten years.

## Quizzle

**Which of these French words or phrases are real?**

- *Amuse-bouche* – A light appetizer (literally "mouth pleaser")

- *Louis de freuer* – An impairment (literally "broken foot")

- *Coup de grâce* – A finishing strike (literally "a blow of mercy")

- *Raison d'être* – Justification of existence (literally "reason for being")

- *Stache silenne* – An assassin (literally "silent mustache")

- *Eau de la croche* – A facial expression of disgust, usually intended for Americans (literally "smells like inner thigh")

*Answers: Amuse-bouche, coup de grâce, and raison d'être are real.*

# Yo momma is such a **sybarite**, she makes Liberace look **ascetic**!

**syb·a·rite** (SIHB uh rite)
n. A person seeking luxury and pleasure

Someone who is a **sybarite** surrounds him or herself with luxurious things and never passes up a chance to be self-indulgent. Yo **sybaritic** momma might sprinkle caviar on her breakfast as if it were pepper. She drives a luxury car with state of the art GPS, a climate control center, and fine Corinthian leather seats; and most likely, she pushes her baby around in a stroller with the same features. Her sheets are of a thread count **ineffably** (see p. 14) high. A sybarite is similar to a **hedonist** (see p. 83), but with an emphasis on luxury. Where a hedonist might like to rock and roll all night and party ev-e-ry day, a sybarite would like to rock and roll all night with the best instruments in existence, and party ev-e-ry day with Spago catering and Dom Perignon champagne.

**as·cet·ic** (uh SET ik)
adj. Denying oneself any and all forms of indulgence
n. An ascetic person

Don't bother getting your **ascetic** momma a nice gift for her birthday. She won't accept it. Ascetic as she is, she'll deny herself pretty much anything that might make her life more comfortable or pleasurable. Maybe yo momma is trying to emulate monks who live ascetic lives, depriving themselves of material possessions so they can concentrate on spiritual fulfillment. Whatever the case, yo momma has made the conscious choice to be **indigent** (see p. 49). Ascetic can be a noun as well, meaning someone who is ascetic. As in: Ascetics live **austere** (self-disciplined, without excess) lifestyles.

Knowing how to use words can be the difference between being Don Juan and Don Rickles. Which of the following pick-up lines are flattering, and which ones might get a drink thrown in your face?

1. "Good thing I'm not **acrophobic**, because you send me straight to heaven."

2. "You are the **apotheosis** of beauty!"

3. "I bet you get asked out by a lot of **masochists**."

4. "You must be a **mountebank** because you've **purloined** (stolen) my heart"

5. "Of all the women in here, you are by far the most **epicene**."

6. "Maybe it's just the **diaphanous** veil of inebriation, but you look like a ten."

7. "Even a monk would have a difficult time being **ascetic** around you."

8. "Has anyone ever told you that you are an **epigone** of Angelina Jolie?"

9. "If you give me a chance, I promise to give you the most **soporific** night of your life!"

_Answers: 1. flattering 2. flattering 3. insulting 4. insulting 5. insulting 6. insulting 7. flattering 8. tough to say 9. just pathetic_

**Yo momma** is so exceedingly large in size that when she sits around the house, idling without intention or activity of any particular sort in the general vicinity of her abode, she in fact literally sits AROUND the house, in that her preposterously expansive material components ooze forth from said domestic residence and then circumscribe the aforementioned living quarters in an undulating moat of flesh, a veritable torus of corpulence!

**verb·ose** (vur BOHS)
adj. A long-winded and wordy style not easily subject to loss of breath and given to prosy rambling that is characterized by a superfluous and vexing propensity of the needless use of many or too many ineffectually pompous and tediously long, drawn-out observations made in the most excessive of styles and delivered in a manner that implies a lavish loquaciousness, garrulity, or dullness often referred to as—drum roll, please—diarrhea of the mouth.

If ugly were bricks, **yo momma** would be a **bastion**!

**bas·tion** (BASS chuhn)
n. A place protected against attack

A **bastion** is a stronghold where people can go for protection during a battle, a kind of fortress. Bastion is most often used figuratively, meaning something that protects a quality or principle: "*Frontline* is a bastion of integrity in today's biased media." If ugly were bricks, yo momma could also be a **bulwark**, which is a protective wall. Choosing which word to use is often a matter of taste. Luckily, yo momma's so ugly that if ugly were bricks, she could be both a bulwark and bastion, and still have bricks left over for an outdoor **rampart** (surrounding wall).

# Yo Momma's
# Gratuitous Product Placement:

**Yo momma's** so dumb, she thought Taco Bell was a Mexican phone company!

**Yo momma's** so stupid, you can tell when she's used the computer because there's Liquid Paper® all over the screen.

**Yo momma** doesn't wear Levi's 501's; she wears 1002's!

> **gra·tu·i·tous** (gruh TOO i tuss)
> adj. Unwarranted, present or displayed for no reason

The growing popularity of TiVo and other digital video recorders (which allow viewers to eliminate commercials) has caused networks to create a new **paradigm** (model) of television advertising, weaving more name-brand products into the storylines of popular television shows. The inclusion of the products is not always warranted by the material, and art is becoming an excuse to promote products. This phenomenon has been criticized as **gratuitous** product placement (see the following page).

In general, if something's gratuitous, it has no real reason for being there. It's unnecessary, but in a different way from **superfluous** (see p. 86). If something is superfluous, it's extra, excess. If something is gratuitous, it really has no business being there in the first place. Parents object to gratuitous violence in video games and gratuitous nudity in movies. At times, the authors of this book provide pop culture references for a purpose, and other times, the references are just gratuitous. If you insult someone (or his or her momma) for no reason, you've hurled a gratuitous insult.

# LAW AND ORDER: GPP
## Gratuitous Product Placement:

**EXT. NEW YORK STREET - DAY**

Detectives CASSADY and GREEN walk down the street.
They examine a dead body in front of them. The dead
body wears a jacket that clearly reads Nike, along with
Nike shoes.

> GREEN
> He sure loved his Nike.

> CASSADY
> Question is, "Who just did it?"

Cassady takes out a Baby Ruth and takes a bite.

> GREEN
> Thought you were on a diet.

> CASSADY
> Baby Ruth has less fat than most candy bars...
> Call forensics, let's see what they can turn up.

CLOSE ON Cassady taking a big bite of his Baby Ruth.

**INT. FORENSICS LAB - DAY**

Cassady and Green talk to the FORENSICS TECHNICIAN.

> TECHNICIANS
> We found something interesting.

> CASSADY
> More interesting than the taste of peanuts and
> chocolate? I'd like to hear that.

TECHNICIANS
The knives used in the stabbing were Cutco knives.

She pulls out a set of knives.

CASSADY
(looking at it) Sharp.

TECHNICIAN
They never lose their edge.

GREEN
No pun intended.

TECHNICIAN
Cut right through bone and muscle.

CASSADY
Impressive.

Another LAB TECHNICIAN enters. He wears a FUBU
JUMPSUIT, eats from a box of Apple Jacks, and listens to
an iPod.

TECHNICIAN 2
(singing)
Doo Doo Doo Doo Doo Doo TJ Maxx!

# Yo Momma's Tasty Leftovers

## Yo momma's so lachrymose, she uses a quilt for a handkerchief!

**lach•ry•mose** (LAK ri mohs)
adj. Sorrowful, inclined to tears; causing tears

Yo **lachrymose** momma sheds more tears than a guest on a Barbara Walters special. The last five minutes of *Grey's Anatomy* often features characters' lachrymose confessions, resulting in a rainstorm of lachrymose viewers.

## Yo momma is so vindictive, she smacked you when you were born for the labor pains you put her through.

**vin•dic•tive** (vin DIK tihv)
n. Inclined to seek revenge; motivated by spite

Yo **vindictive** momma holds onto a grudge. Vengeful and spiteful by nature, she doesn't like to let things go, and takes the necessary action to get revenge and injure those who injured her.

## Yo momma's grasp on reality is so tenuous, when she went to take the 44 bus, she took the 22 twice.

**ten•u•ous**
adj. Thin, unsubstantial, lacking a solid foundation (regarding reasoning or understanding)

**Tenuous** can mean slender, as in "tenuous thread," or can mean thin in a more figurative sense. Understandings, arguments, and grasps are tenuous in this sense.

# Yo momma's so **didactic**, she corrects her doctor's penmanship!

**di·dac·tic** (dye DAK tik)
adj. Heavy-handedly or condescendingly instructive; overly prone to lecture others

Ever noticed how the last five minutes of nature shows is usually a downer? We've been following monkeys through the jungle for 55 minutes, but then it's time to show a bunch of guys with chainsaws cutting trees down and clearing the forest. The message – nature is precious – is fine, but the means, we can say, is **didactic**. That is, there's a whiff of moralizing instruction in the bummer endings, and nobody likes that.

# Yo momma's so **moribund**, she's hosting the new *Tales from the Crypt*.

**mor·i·bund** (MORE i buhnd)
adj. Dying, approaching death; in a decline toward extinction

If you're a person and you're **moribund**, you're dying. If something that's not a person is moribund, it's not necessarily dying: It's not developing or showing any vitality, like a sports team that all the other schools play for homecoming, or Steve Guttenberg's movie career. You can describe dead-end relationships as moribund, for the most part. Moribund is not **morbid**. Morbid indicates an unhealthy preoccupation with death and/or disease. That is, yo momma has this hosting job because her predecessor on *Tales from the Crypt* was a skeleton, and yo momma's getting close to skeletonhood herself; she's not hosting it because of an odd obsession she has with people getting knocked off by drifters.

# Yo momma is attractive, smart, and young… on Antithesis Day!

**an·ti·the·sis** (an TIH thuh sis)
n. Direct opposite

You use this word when you want a little more juice than "opposite." As in, "Yo momma's face is the **antithesis** of beauty."

**Some words and their antitheses:**

**Word: abstemious** (ab STEM ee uhs)
adj. Showing restraint in indulgences, especially food or drink
**Antithesis: hedonistic** (see p. 82)

**Word: pejorative** (puh JOHR uh tiv)
adj. Belittling, insulting
n. A belittling remark
**Antithesis: complimentary, laudatory** (see p. 25)

**Word: surreptitious** (sur ep TISH us)
adj. Marked by stealth
**Antithesis: blatant** (BLAYT nt)
adj. Totally obvious

**Gratuitous** (see p. 135) picture of a wooden duck.

Yo momma is a **voracious** (see p. 3) reader. She reads everything, even titles at the **nadir** (bottommost point) of the sales sheet. In doing so, yo momma equips herself with an arsenal of interesting new words and new ideas. Below are some worst-selling books and the corresponding words yo momma learned from them.

### Fallen Brave
*An Indian is exiled from his tribe when his rain dance contains too many lewd, provocative gestures*

This Indian is an **iconoclast**. An iconoclast (eye KAHN uh klast) is someone who defies tradition. **Iconoclasm** not only veers from tradition, but, in doing so, attacks the sacredness of cherished beliefs and practices.

### Where's Waldo – Great War Series
*Interactive book where young readers try to find Waldo in great battles of history amidst anonymous deaths and bloodshed*

This book is **macabre**. If something is macabre, it is dark and gruesome, and often related to death. Macabre is unusual in that it can be pronounced with the third syllable (muh CAHB ruh) or without it (muh CAHB), as if you just got sick of saying the word half way through.

### Best of Emergency Broadcast Tests (Audio Book)
*A collection of classic prolonged **strident** (see p. 25) tones*

This audio book is **monotonous**. Monotonous can mean "not changing pitch or inflection" (just one note). This audio tape is also monotonous in the broader sense, meaning "tediously repetitious." Monotonous things are boring because they have no variety. Practicing scales is monotonous. To many, NASCAR is monotonous; the cars just go around and around and around. Until this book, learning vocabulary was monotonous.

# Esoteric ⟨Yo Momma⟩ Jokes

> **esoteric** (ESS oh tair ik)
> adj. Meant for or understood by a select few with specialized knowledge

If something is **esoteric**, it is not meant for everyone. You can feel the whiff as it goes over your head. Esoteric knowledge is accessible only to the "enlightened few." Sometimes the enlightened few are the highly educated, while other times, they are those with a specialized knowledge, as is the case with the esoteric yo momma jokes below:

## Cheesemakers - **Yo momma's** so **putrid**
(see p. 15), she makes Vieux-Boulogne smell like Robiola Rocchetta!

## Astrologists - **Yo momma's** so mean, she
makes a Scorpio with her moon in Taurus look like a Pisces with Gemini rising!

## Balloonist Aficionados (enthusiasts) -
**Yo momma's** so fat, Phileas Fogg couldn't **circumnavigate** (see p. 127) her in 80 days!

## Mathematicians -
**Yo momma** $= x+y(e{:}86) -y^2+z56{:}>y+9\{z^{45}\} =$ fat

**Bacteriologists** - **Yo Momma** is so nasty, Anton van Leeuwenhoek would've had a field day discovering new things on her!

**Cryptographers** - **ZB OBOOC** HJ JB JKERHX, JFP ACG'K PIPG XPABXP KFHJ JHORQP AYZRKBTYCO!  (You can actually decode this.)

**Venetian Gondoliers** - *O' Voste Momma...* ♪ ♫
♫ *È molto grassa... avete saputo... lei affondata la barca!?* ♪ ♪

**Ophthalmologists**

Y
O M
O M M
A I S S
O N E A R
S I G H T E
D T H A T S H
E U S E S T H E H
U B B L E T E L E S C O
P E A S A C O N T A C T L E N S

# Yo momma's so lethargic, she gets enervated from slogging up the stairs.

**le•thar•gic** (luh THAR jik)
adj. Listless and unenergetic

Yo **lethargic** momma is a big mound of sluggishness. She's got the energy of a wake. She's a yawn personified, a black hole of lazy **apathy** (see p. 88). Yo momma's **lethargy** causes her to live a **sedentary** (see p. 113) life in body and mind, and every movement is a profound effort that seems to **enervate** her.

**en•er•vate** (EN er vate)
v. To sap the vitality of, either physically or mentally

To **enervate** is to weaken, to sap the strength of. It's important to know this word, as it vaguely resembles one almost its opposite—in this case, "energize." Evil SAT designers relish a word like this. When you're **enervated**, you're pooped, exhausted. It's acceptable to use it to describe something that weakens you mentally or emotionally, too: "This relationship drama is just plain **enervating**."

**slog** (SLOG)
v. To walk heavily and slowly

Writers will tell you that the verb is the most powerful part of speech. An example should make this obvious: It's better to say "The old man scowled at me" than to say "The old man's wrinkled face became more wrinkled as his wide eyes became more narrow, his anger increasing." You can pile adjective on top of adjective, but straightforward and descriptive noun-verb combinations can't be topped. Consider how descriptive the word **slog** is. Yo momma doesn't just walk up the stairs. She slogs. She **trudges**. She **plods**. She doesn't skip, or dance, or **trundle**. She slogs. "Slog" even has some **onomatopoeia** (see p. 99) to it. What yo momma is doing somehow sounds like she is "**slogging**."

# Yo Momma's Street Smarts

## Ways To **Extricate** Yourself From a Telemarketing Pitch

**ex·tri·cate** (EK stri kate)
v. To free from entanglement (as in a difficult situation)

If a **telemarketer** calls you and refuses to let you get off the phone, there are ways you can extricate yourself from the situation. All you have to do is confuse them, or maybe scare them a little. Use any of the following techniques:

- Unprompted, tell them what you are wearing.

- Battle rap with them.

- Speak in an indecipherable Scottish accent.

- Inquire ardently about their weight, address, sign, and "openness to new ideas."

- Phase in and out of robotspeak.

- Laugh at everything they say, sometimes escalating your admiration into applause.

- If they ask, "Do you live alone?" You answer, "Do voices count?"

- Assume they are your friend, Mitchell. Do not accept otherwise.

- Refuse to cooperate unless telemarketer does a duet of "Memories" with you.

- Sob uncontrollably, go into a long tangent about the break-up of your barber shop quartet group.

- Answer their questions, but at the end of your responses, subtly add, "Resistance is futile."

- Politely tell them, 'I'm sorry. I have no free will."

# A Review of **Yo Momma**

Yo Momma has taught you well. But how well? The following pages test your understanding of the words in *Yo Momma*. If you need to review a word, look in the **index** (p. 161), where you'll find a complete list of words along with their corresponding page numbers.

**1. Yo momma's** so _____, she makes a mime look loquacious!

 a. **garrulous**    c. **taciturn**

 b. **apathetic**    d. **jaundiced**

**2. Yo momma's** so _____, she lost a quarter in a wrinkle.

 a. **wizened**    c. **mortified**

 b. **sanguine**    d. **Leonard Maltin**

**3. Yo momma's** so _____, she dreams in black and white.

 a. **pallid**    c. **antediluvian**

 b. **penurious**    d. **fudgeriffic**

**4. Yo momma's** wrists are so _____, she has to connect two wristwatches around one arm!

 a. **distended**    c. **anodyne**

 b. **turgid**    d. **both a and b**

*Answers: 1c; 2a; 3c; 4d*

**5.** Match the horrible cell phone ring setting to the word(s) that best describes it.

    a. Wet Hacking Cough     **Lachrymose**

    b. Sulfur Emission     **Egregiously** painful

    c. Taser     **Fetid**

    d. Obituary     **Cacophonous**

**6.** Match the children's book/show character with the trait it irresponsibly celebrates.

    a. Flat Stanley     **Morbid corpulence**

    b. Cookie Monster     **Emaciation**

    c. Fat Albert     **Voraciousness**

    d. Tom and Jerry     **Macabre** violence

**7.** Match the onomatopoeia with the corresponding animal word.

    a. Oink     **Lupine**

    b. Roar     **Porcine**

    c. Moo     **Leonine, Ursine**

    d. Howl     **Bovine**

**8.** Match the emoticon with the word is most closely expresses.

    a.     **Lachrymose**

    b.     **Sanguine**

    c.     **Taciturn**

    d.     **Ambivalent**

Answers: 5. a) cacophonous; b) fetid; c) egregiously painful; d) lachrymose 6. a) emaciation; b) voraciousness; c) morbid corpulence; d) macabre violence 7. a) porcine; b) leonine, ursine c) bovine; d)lupine 8. a) sanguine; b) lachrymose; c) ambivalent; d) taciturn

**Test your reading comprehension with the following story:**

Once upon a time, there was yo momma. **Yo momma** was so **diminutive**, she had to stand on her toes to get the mail. In addition, her legs were incorrigibly **hirsute**. Any effort to **depilate** them was quickly met with a newly **burgeoning** crop. So yo momma decided to comb the long hair under her **turgid**, **fetid**, and **callous** feet to make her taller.

**9.** According to the story above, **yo momma** is the **antithesis** of _____.

    a. **maudlin**　　　　c. **Brobdingnagian**

    b. **mellifluous**　　　d. **Simon Bolivar**

**10.** The hair on **yo momma's** legs could best be described as _____.

    a. **delectable**　　　c. **diaphanous**

    b. **copious**　　　　　d. **Stamos-like**

**11.** To say **yo momma** is "not the smoothest ice cube in the freezer" is a(n) _____.

    a. **euphemism**　　　c. **simile**

    b. **paradigm**　　　　d. **neologism**

**12.** If this **lachrymose** tale of **yo momma** made you well up with compassionate tears, you felt this story had _____.

    a. **bathos**　　　　　c. **wathos**

    b. **pathos**　　　　　d. **afros**

**Choose the words that best complete the sentence.**

**13.** When Jake ditched the neighborhood kids who were making a movie using a Super 8 digital camera, and instead went into the woods with a bowie knife strapped to his leg, vowing to return with "some pelts," the neighborhood kids said, "Hey, Jake, don't be such a _____. Can't you see that your way of living is growing more and more _____?"

a) **sinecure**; **sanguine**   c) **termagant**; **pallid**

b) **Luddite**; **senescent**   d) **Billy Ray Cyrus**; **jaundiced**

**14.** After years of being henpecked by his ancient landlord—whose skin appeared to have devoured every ray of sun in Arizona decades ago and who berated him at every opportunity—Wally summoned up the courage to call her a _____ _____ (2 words).

a) **wizened harridan**   d) **Charles Barkley**

b) **wizened termagant**   e) **a, b, c**

c) **wizened virago**   f) **all of the above**

**15.** You just got a job that pays you $400,000 a year to test-drive Ferraris. In the hills of the Italian Alps. Whenever you want, because hey, sometimes you've gotta go skiing. Your job is a(n) _____.

a) **epitome**   c) **sinecure**

b) **hoovie**   d) **blandishment**

*Answers: 13b; 14e; 15c.*

# No Wrong Answers

**16.** Worst name for a boy band:

- **Schadenfreude**
- **Ad Hoc**
- The **Taciturn** Ten
- The **Mountebanks**

**17.** What is your favorite made-up **portmanteau** word?

- **Hudge** – Fudge-covered ham
- **Grandmothra** – A Japanese monster who always sends you $5 on your birthday
- **Gapple** – The time that passes between your reservation at the Genius Bar and when you actually are helped
- **TsarJones** – Name for the couple if Star Jones exhumed Tsar Nicholas II

**18.** Which is the most **nauseous** ice cream flavor?

- Salmon Chunk
- Bubble Gum (with already chewed wads)
- Dirty Coins N' Cream
- Linty Minty

**19.** What is the worst sports team nickname (as in Jets, Giants, Celtics, etc.)?

- The **Viragos**
- The **Wizened** Wizards
- The **Specious** Reasoning
- The Fighting **Sampletons**

**Choose the words that best complete the sentence.**

20. _____ alongside Verne Troyer (Mini Me), Spud Webb, one of the smaller players in NBA history, looks positively _____.

   a) **Juxtaposed**; **Brobdingnagian**
   b) **Belied**; **atavistic**
   c) **Prostrated**; **pyrrhic**
   d) **Aflame**; **vulpine**

21. Some say that after professors attain tenure, their attention to teaching wanes and becomes a _____ effort.

   a) **troglodytic**          c) **perfunctory**
   b) **spicy candy**         d) **ostentatious**

22. Rob is totally _____, so when he heard that there was such a thing as a toilet that doubles as an aquarium, he said "No way."

   a) **epicene**             c) **incredulous**
   b) **prostrate**           d) **fly**

23. After the fire department hired the arsonist, the local paper properly called it a(n) _____ mistake.

   a) **distended**           d) **rapacious**
   b) **polygamous**         e) **Isiah Thomas**
   c) **egregious**

*Answers: 20a; 21c; 22c (Note: Google "Fish 'n Flush"); 23c*

**24. Yo momma's** so _____, her face is on the front of a food stamp.

 a. **indigent**     c. **tacit**

 b. **superfluous**    d. **adhesive**

**25. Yo momma's** so _____, she asked for a price check at the 99 cent store.

 a. **timorous**     c. **some of the above**

 b. **vestigial**     d. **obtuse**

**26.** If **yo momma** can shave her back without using a mirror, she is both _____, and _____.

 a. **hirsute, esophoric**

 b. **hirsute, loquacious**

 c. **vociferous, esophoric**

 d. **specious, Eli Whitney**

**27. Yo momma's** so _____, she has to run around in the shower to get wet.

 a) **homely**

 b) **unctuous**

 c) **fetid**

 d) **emaciated**

**28.** Answer "True," "False," or "Harriet Tubman" for the following statements.

a. **Soporific** things are helpful to wake you up in the mornings.

b. Troglodytes are **clairvoyant** in their ability to spot new trends.

c. She created the underground railroad.

d. Laughing at someone who trips off a stage on *America's Funniest Videos* is a form of **schadenfreude**.

e. "No one can eye ere no one tac on" is a **palindrome**.

f. Born into slavery in 1819 or 1820, in Dorchester County, Maryland.

g. **Verbose** and **laconic** are opposites.

h. If you are **veracious**, you have an **insatiable** appetite.

i. If you want to tan your **pallid** stomach, you should lie **prostrate**.

j. This statement is a **paradox**.

k. Sneezing into your shirt pocket during a formal dinner is **gauche**.

l. **Gamines** are **gluttonous**.

m. These Harriet Tubman facts are **gratuitous**.

*Answers: a) False; b) False; c) Harriet Tubman; d) True; e) False (check it); f) Harriet Tubman; g) True; h) False; i) False; j) False; k) True; l) False; m) True. But if they are gratuitous that means that they help illustrate the word "gratuitous" in conjunction with this statement, so they are not gratuitous, so this statement is false. But if they are not gratuitous, then they do not have any reason to be here, so they are gratuitous, but if… paradox… too hard to comprehend… does not compute… Overload!… Overload!… Overload… Overloooooooaaaaaaad!*

**Test your reading comprehension with the following story:**

There once was **yo momma**. Yo momma lived a **sedentary** life, sitting around eating **ravenously** and watching **asinine** television. She had an **indefatigable lethargy**. One day, she tired of **slogging** through the **monotonous ennui** of her life and took a stroll. Yo rather **corpulent** momma liked to wear **ostentatious** high-heeled shoes. When she took a step, she struck oil.

**29.** The phrase "**indefatigable lethargy**" is an example of a(n) _____.

    a. **eponym**       c. **oxymoron**

    b. **epithet**       d. **good racehorse name**

**30.** If yo momma's high heel struck oil, it must have punctured the ground to _____ depths.

    a. **execrable**       c. **impalpable**

    b. **abysmal**       d. **pallid**

**31.** In this passage, **monotonous** means the opposite of _____.

    a. **Jingoistic**

    b. **Penurious**

    c. **Mercurial**

    d. **Monobrow**

## 32. Sybarite or Ascetic?

a. Donald Trump

b. Gandhi

c. MC Hammer circa 1986

d. The weird dude who went off into the forest with a sack of rice

## 33. Impassive or Effusive?

a. Keanu Reeves in *The Matrix*

b. **Obsequious** *E!* interviews

c. Native American stereotypes

d. William Shatner's acting

## 34. Parasite or Saprophyte?

The following people are either alive or dead. If you feed off of them, would you be a parasite or a saprophyte?

a. Joe Piscopo

b. Nell Carter

c. Mayim Bialik

d. Milli

e. Vanilli

f. Dracula

*Answers: 32. a) ascetic; b) sybarite; c) sybarite; d) ascetic 33. a) impassive; b) effusive; c) impassive; d) effusive 34. a) parasite; b) saprophyte; c) saprophyte; d) parasite; e) saprophyte; f) technically "undead," so the jury is still out on this one.*

## ( **Battle Rap** )

Uh oh! You just got challenged to a battle rap! You need to bust some killer rhymes if you plan gain the respect of the inner city Detroit locals and move away from your alcoholic trailer park mother who looks exactly like Kim Basinger. The stakes are high!

**35.** Replace the phrase in bold with the correct word from the list below.

Words: defenestration, emaciation, castigation, depilation

> **Yo momma's** *severe scolding*
> Of your daddy's *lack of hair*
> And your sister's *extreme skinniness*
> Led to her *being pushed out the window*.

**36.** Replace the phrase in bold with the correct word from the list below.

Words: enervated, equivocated, prostrated,

> **Yo daddy** *spoke in a purposefully unclear and*
>    *confusing manner*
> Till he became so *weak and drained of energy*
> And he collapsed *face down on the ground*.

**37.** "Yo momma's face looks like a blocked punt" is an
example of a(n) _____.

    a. **acronym**         c. **simile**

    b. **eponym**          d. **sampleton**

**38.** If yo momma is prone to digressions, you may say her
brain is _____.

    a. **peripatetic**

    b. **sanguine**

    c. **sornitated**

    d. **banal**

**39.** If you're looking for a cheerful paint, what is your best bet?

    a. **jaundice**

    b. **pallid**

    c. **sanguine**

    d. **fetid**

**40.** Which answer is a **paradox**?

    a. both a and b

    b. neither a nor b

    c. this is way too confusing (circuit malfunction!)

    d. all of the above

# No Wrong Answers

**41.** Which of things are better **depilated** and which are better **hirsute**?

- Joey Lawrence's head
- A man's chest
- Tom Selleck's philtrum

**42.** Which show is best for a dose of **schadenfreude**?

- *Breaking Bonaduce*
- *American Idol*
- George Bush press conferences

**43.** What is **anathema** to you?

- People who don't signal
- Smoking
- **Verbose** books

**44.** Pick the word that best describes the way you are taking this quiz.

- **Insouciantly**
- **Perfunctorily**
- **Meticulously**

**45.** Worst name for a gangsta rapper: Alakritee, Sangwyn, or Ambivuhlint?

**46.** Worst name for a car: Dodge Reprobate, Chevy Martinet, or Mercedes Weltschmerz?

**47. Yo momma's** so _____, she made an onion cry.

   a. **homely**

   b. **comely**

   c. **succulent**

   d. **unctuous**

**48. Yo momma's** so _____, she can watch a tennis match without moving her head.

   a. **acrophobic**

   b. **megalomaniacal**

   c. **monomaniacal**

   d. **esophoric**

**49. Yo momma's** so _____, she sweats Crisco.

   a. **lucid**

   b. **diaphanous**

   c. **maudlin**

   d. **unctuous**

**50. Yo momma's** breath is so _____, when she yawns, her teeth duck.

   a. **putrid**

   b. **fetid**

   c. **noisome**

   d. **all of the above**

*Answers: 47a; 48d; 49d; 50d*

# Index aka "The **Yo Momma Lexicon**"

**lexicon** (LEKS i kahn)
n. A stock of terms used in a particular profession, subject, or style; a vocabulary

# About the Authors

**Justin Heimberg** first used *The Yo Momma Vocabulary Builder* as an exercise while teaching a writing workshop in a juvenile detention center in Los Angeles, where his literally captive audience had no choice but to suffer through his humor. Justin is a professional comedy writer who has written movies for most of the major Hollywood studios. He is the author of many books with not so many words, and has written humor for *Esquire*, *Details*, and *MAD*.

**Christopher Schultz** has written for *The New York Times*, the *New York Sun*, and *Spin*, among other publications. His fiction has appeared in *Esquire*, *Shenandoah*, and on his floor. He is the founder of Start Here Project Development, a consultancy that strengthens the communications of universities, nonprofits, and businesses.

**Steve Harwood** first started insulting yo momma in college as a way to entertain underprivileged liberal arts students in need of improv comedy. He is a stand-up comedian and screenwriter who is currently very popular in the future.

## About Classless Education

Classless Education is a collective of comedy writers and educators who believe that learning should be a part of life, not apart from it.

**For more about Classless Education's mission, products, and services, check out**
## classlesseducation.com